The Shakespeare Handbooks

WITHDRAWN

THE SHAKESPEARE HANDBOOKS

Series Editor: John Russell Brown

PUBLISHED

FORTHCOMING

The Shakespeare Handbooks

The Winter's Tale

Ros King

palgrave
macmillan

First published 2009 by
PALGRAVE MACMILLAN

Palgrave Macmillan in the UK is an imprint of Macmillan Publishers Limited, registered in England, company number 785998, of Houndmills, Basingstoke, Hampshire RG21 6XS.

Palgrave Macmillan in the US is a division of St Martin's Press LLC, 175 Fifth Avenue, New York, NY 10010.

Palgrave Macmillan is the global academic imprint of the above companies and has companies and representatives throughout the world.

Palgrave® and Macmillan® are registered trademarks in the United States, the United Kingdom, Europe and other countries.

ISBN-13: 978-0-230-00851-9   hardback
ISBN-10: 0-230-00851-8   hardback
ISBN-13: 978-0-230-00852-6   paperback
ISBN-10: 0-230-00852-6   paperback

This book is printed on paper suitable for recycling and made from fully managed and sustained forest sources. Logging, pulping and manufacturing processes are expected to conform to the environmental regulations of the country of origin.

A catalogue record for this book is available from the British Library.

Library of Congress Cataloging-in-Publication Data

King, Ros.
  The winter's tale / Ros King.
    p. cm. — (The Shakespeare handbooks)
  Includes index.
  ISBN-13: 978-0-230-00851-9
  ISBN-10: 0-230-00851-8
  ISBN-13: 978-0-230-00852-6 (pbk.)
  ISBN-10: 0-230-00852-6 (pbk.)
  1. Shakespeare, William, 1564–1616. Winter's tale—Handbooks, manuals, etc. 2. Shakespeare, William, 1564–1616—Dramatic production—Handbooks, manuals, etc. 3. Shakespeare, William, 1564–1616—Film and video adaptations—Handbooks, manuals, etc. I. Title. II. Series: Shakespeare handbooks (Palgrave Macmillan (Firm))

PR2839.K56 2009
822.3'3 — dc22   2008038446

10 9 8 7 6 5 4 3 2 1
18 17 16 15 14 13 12 11 10 09

Printed and bound in China

For Daughters near and far

Contents

General Editor's Preface

The Shakespeare Handbooks provide an innovative way of studying the plays in performance. The commentaries, which are their core feature, enable a reader to envisage the words of a text unfurling in performance, involving actions and meanings not readily perceived except in rehearsal or performance. The aim is to present the plays in the environment for which they were written and to offer an experience as close as possible to an audience's progressive experience of a production.

While each book has the same range of contents, their authors have been encouraged to shape them according to their own critical and scholarly understanding and their first-hand experience of theatre practice. The various chapters are designed to complement the commentaries: the cultural context of each play is presented together with quotations from original sources; the authority of its text or texts is considered with what is known of the earliest performances; key performances and productions of its subsequent stage history are both described and compared. The aim in all this has been to help readers to develop their own informed and imaginative view of a play in ways that supplement the provision of standard editions and are more user-friendly than detailed stage histories or collections of criticism from diverse sources.

Further volumes are in preparation so that, within a few years, the Shakespeare Handbooks will be available for all the plays that are frequently performed and studied.

John Russell Brown

Acknowledgements

Sections from the Commentary to Act I and Key Productions have appeared as parts of two other articles: 'Reading Beyond Words: Sound and Gesture in The Winter's Tale' in *Pedagogy* vol. 7.3, 2007 and 'Dramaturgy: beyond the presentism/historicism dichotomy' *Shakespearean International Yearbook*, Vol. 5, Ashgate, 2007. I am grateful to these journal editors for permission to republish, to Roger Lowman for commenting on aspects of the manuscript, and to Maria Hayward for alerting me to royal funeral effigies.

All references to this play and other works of Shakespeare are to *The Complete Works* edited by Stanley Wells and Gary Taylor, Oxford: Clarendon Press, 1986.

1 The Text and Early Performances

The only early version of the text of *The Winter's Tale* is that printed seven years after Shakespeare's death in the 1623 First Folio of his works. Certain features of this text, including the heavy, 'literary' style of its punctuation, suggest that the manuscript from which it was printed was not in Shakespeare's hand, but had been copied, probably by the scribe Ralph Crane. Shakespeare, in common with many poets, probably punctuated quite lightly. Heavy punctuation can sometimes break up rhetorical patterns and therefore get in the way of actors' performances. There are few overt problems with the words of the play, however, and those that have a bearing on the sense or on performance are considered in the Commentary section below as they occur.

One particularly problematic aspect of the Folio text's punctuation in all the plays is its extensive use of the colon. In his book *The Petie Schole* (1587), Francis Clement described the colon as 'holding forth the voice likewise at the pause of silence in expectation of as much more to be spoken as is already rehearsed' (p. 25). In other words, although a colon was used to indicate a slight pause in the voice, it was regarded as a mark of connection between two parts of a sentence. Modern editors have often substituted full stops in an attempt to make long speeches more manageable, but these tend to separate rather than connect, and the effect is often to make the text more difficult to understand.

The other problem particularly relating to this text in the Folio is that the scribe has minimised stage directions, mostly reducing them to lists of speaking parts at the head of each scene. Thus the entrance to II.i is given as *Enter Hermione, Mamillius, Ladies: Leontes, Antigonus, Lords.* The colon here marks two groupings, without stipulating clearly that Leontes's group should enter later. Similarly the succession of exits and entrances in II.ii and the presence there of non-speaking attendants, all of whom are specifically demanded by the dialogue, are not accounted for in the blanket stage direction at the head of the scene, which gives merely *Enter Paulina, a Gentleman, Gaoler, Emilia*.

The stage directions that are commonly supplied by modern editors tend to follow those first inserted by the seventeenth and eighteenth century editors Nicholas Rowe and Lewis Theobald and can sometimes preserve their sense of decorum and social status. For example, editorial stage directions in II.ii treat the Gentleman as if he were accompanying Paulina, thus providing moral security for a lone aristocratic woman. It is perfectly possible, however, and rather more interesting, if he is regarded as one of the prison officers, in which case a different set of stage directions needs to be supplied (see pp. 20–21).

It is quite unusual to have any firm indication of Shakespeare's plays in performance during his lifetime. Remarkably, we have three such references for *The Winter's Tale*: one at the Globe on 15 May 1611, its story described in some detail by the astrologer and physician Simon Forman; and two records of payment for performances at court on 5 November 1611, and during the winter of 1612–13. This does not mean, of course, that these were the earliest actual performances in either venue and later sections of this book will argue that the play was probably written for performance at court during the winter of 1610–11. Unusually, the play retained its suitability for court performance, being seen there at least twice more before 1624 and again ten years later.

Simon Forman and the Globe performance, 15 May 1611

There was no such professional discipline as theatre criticism in the early seventeenth century. The few eyewitness accounts of performances that have come down to us therefore tend to be anecdotal rather than analytical and to remark merely on those aspects of the performance that seemed important to the writer on a personal level. Forman is no exception. He saw four plays in a short space of time in early 1611, shortly before he died, which he recorded in a manuscript headed *Booke of Plaies and Notes thereof per formans for Common Pollicie*. All four of these descriptions have Shakespearean sounding titles, but probably only three relate to actual Shakespearean plays: *Macbeth, Cymbeline* and *The Winter's Tale*. In each case he seems to be remembering details as he writes, which sometimes results in a telling of the story which is neither chronological nor exactly in the order presented in the play.

> Observe there how Leontes, the king of Sicilia, was overcome with jealousy of his wife with the king of Bohemia, his friend that came to see him; and how he contrived his death and would have had his cupbearer to have poisoned, who gave the king of Bohemia warning thereof and fled with him to Bohemia.
>
> Remember also how he sent to the Oracle of Apollo, and the answer of Apollo, that she was guiltless and that the king was jealous, etc, and how except the child was found again that was lost, the king should die without issue; for the child was carried into Bohemia and there laid in a forest and brought up by a shepherd. And the king of Bohemia his son married that wench, and how they fled into Sicilia to Leontes; and the shepherd having showed the letter of the noble man by whom Leontes sent away that child and the jewels found about her, she was known to be Leontes's daughter, and was then sixteen years old.
>
> Remember also the rogue that came in all tattered like colt pixie, and how he feigned him sick and to have been robbed of all that he had, and how he cozened the poor man of all his money, and after came to the sheep shear with a peddler's pack and there cozened them again of all their money. And how he changed apparel with the king of Bohemia his son, and then how he turned courtier, etc. Beware of trusting feigned beggars or fawning fellows. [Modernised spelling and punctuation]

Using words like 'observe' or 'remember', Forman only bothers to pick out those aspects of the play that were particularly relevant to him, or which he thought might contribute to an understanding of public 'policy'. As a doctor he was most struck by the importance of the doctor's role in *Macbeth* while, as a keen genealogist, the only aspect of *Cymbeline* that seems to have appealed to him was its use of mythical ancient British history. Interestingly, he forbears to mention the cauldron scene in *Macbeth* or the statue scene in *The Winter's Tale*, leading some commentators to assume that the productions he saw omitted these spectacles. Both these scenes suggest the operation of black magic. Forman had been arrested for the possession of magic books and continued to write copiously on the subject himself (although all but one of his works remained unpublished), but he may not have thought it a useful mark of 'common policy' to dwell on aspects that contravened James I's widely published condemnation of magic. Alternatively, as a serious alchemist and astrologer, he probably thought he had nothing to 'remember' from theatrical simulations.

The fact that the statue is also absent from Shakespeare's main source for the play – the prose romance *Pandosto* by Robert Greene – has led to a suggestion that the scene was not part of Shakespeare's original conception but was added to supply a happy ending for performances at court. The text of the play as we have it, however, demonstrates that adding the statue scene would not have been just a simple matter of tacking on a few hundred lines to the end, while replacing a fully fledged recognition scene between Leontes and Perdita with the comic report by the three Gentlemen. The language and imagery of the statue scene are deeply embedded throughout the play in phrases and images that only become fully explicable in the light of that scene: see, for example, the chain of sometimes slightly surprising images relating to food that culminates in Leontes's line 'let it be an art / Lawful as eating' (V.iii.110–11). Equally, it is only when Paulina presents the statue of Hermione as painted by a skilled human hand, with eyes that seem to have 'motion' (in the artistic sense of 'spirit'), and which even seems to breathe (thus suggesting the operation of magical power) that we can fully realise the significance of her earlier speech:

> if you can bring
> Tincture or lustre in her lip, her eye,
> Heat outwardly or breath within, I'll serve you
> As I would do the gods.
> (III.ii.204, cf V.i.64)

Of course, audiences cannot flick back as readers can. The implications of this language are not intended to be fully understood at the time of hearing, but are part of an intricately worked pattern of textures and correspondences that help create the world of the play – a world in which wonders happen. Wonder too, perhaps, has no place in 'common policy', which would explain why Forman omits the scene, even though it is intrinsic to the play.

2   *Commentary*

ACT I

Act I, scene i

1–34   Like Shakespeare's *Cymbeline*, which was probably written for performance at court in 1609–10, this play begins with a conversation between two courtiers. As in the earlier play, the style of speech is rather elaborate, careful and diplomatic, as befits the status of the speakers. Unlike *Cymbeline*, it is in prose, although it is not easy to read. But, as usually the case with Shakespeare, the difficulties incorporate a wealth of clues for actors and readers; they are designed to influence the pace of the scene and to indicate something of what is to come. They introduce not just the story but also the plot: the way in which that story will be presented, arranged and developed.

Camillo and Archidamus are chief advisers to the Kings of Sicily and Bohemia respectively. Their masters, Leontes and Polixenes, were childhood friends and although they have not seen each other for a long time, and are separated by a 'vast', the great geographical gap between their countries, they have kept up a constant exchange of gifts, letters and diplomatic embassies (ll. 22–31). The Sicilians have been so generously hospitable that Archidamus jokingly fears the Bohemians will have to drug the Sicilian entourage when they make a return visit in the summer so that they will not notice when their entertainment falls short (ll. 23–6).

34 to the end   Perhaps he overdoes the flattery. Perhaps Camillo is a little embarrassed. Perhaps as a result, he begins to tie himself in knots when conversation turns to young Prince Mamillius. Archidamus speaks of the 'unspeakable comfort' (l. 34), the delight beyond words, which Mamillius must bring to the Sicilians. Camillo concurs with the decidedly odd idea that the child is capable of reversing the effects of age, making old people want to stay alive so that they might see him grow up. It is a (slightly satirical) version of the hyperbole of Ben Jonson's Panegyric on the occasion of James I's first visit to the English Parliament in March 1604, in which it was claimed that the people of London were so glad to welcome him that 'Old men were glad their fates till now did last; / And infants, that the hours had made such haste' (Johnson, *Works*, 1616, p. 866). Archidamus's subsequent question makes him backtrack a little, now claiming (rather pointlessly) that the elderly and infirm would be willing to die if they had no other reasons for wanting to live. Archidamus, with diplomatic double-speak, concurs by saying that if the king had no son, the elderly would want to live until he had one, while obliquely referring to the proverb that no one desires to die before their time. There is perhaps something wrong after all. Although the characters do not intend it, and the audience may not yet know the significance of what they have heard, this diplomatic language has voiced something 'unspeakable' (cf. l. 34). In a series of oppositions, of plenty and lack, nearness and absence, death and life, the dialogue has insinuated the idea that time and space can be both stretched and collapsed. It has introduced a drugged cup given in name of friendship, suggested that what looks like friendship and generosity can appear to be rivalry and debt when viewed from another angle, and it has linked Mamillius and death.

Act I, scene ii

0.1   Although Folio has given an '*Exeunt*' for Camillo and Archidamus at the end of their dialogue and marks this as a new scene, some editors and many productions roll the two scenes together. F does not mention Camillo in the entrance direction here, but he needs to be on stage later in the scene having observed what has taken place.

1–27   The courtly, elliptical language continues because Polixenes is trying to make his excuses and leave without causing offence, but the manner of his speech again allows us to hear something more complex, and the common production choice that shows us a visibly pregnant Hermione here, although not directly stated either in stage directions or in the dialogue, is probably intended (see pp. 105–6). Even if an audience does not yet fully understand what is happening, the oddity of the language will make us wonder about the significance.

We quickly become aware of a level of conflicting desires in the characters. The surface may be friendly, but Leontes' insistence that Polixenes should stay is 'tougher' (l. 15) than is warranted, even bullying.

Hermione herself is silent at the beginning of the scene, but as we will soon learn, she has a very strong personality. At this moment, she may be interacting with her young son, who in most modern productions is given some kind of toy to play with. Given her lines when she does speak, she is probably observing the conversation between her husband and his friend with some amusement. She is in short an extremely noticeable figure on the stage well before she starts to speak.

27–61 Leontes's terse exclamation, 'Tongue-tied, our Queen?' is not just an invitation to speak, but almost an accusation that Hermione is *not* speaking, as well as a suggestion of the usual male complaint that women speak too much. This is familiar territory in marital argument: the situation that one cannot win, whatever course of action one takes. Hermione reposts by saying that he has been doing it all wrong. The manner of his speaking, his coldness, she says, has provoked Polixenes's refusal (I.ii.28–30). The manner of hers is rather in the ear (and imagination) of the auditor. The later tenor of the play and its treatment of her character means that an actor will want an audience to hear playful teasing, but the repetition of 'sir' and the altercation of 'I' and 'you' allows Leontes to hear Polixenes as the cause of difference between them. Her formality and accusation towards him, playful or not, and her continuing teasing, (over) familiarity towards his friend, her use of oaths and colloquialisms, can only convince him of her guilt. We can see that, although we still also hear her openness.

Together, these aural and visual prompts provide food for the jealous suspicion that is already eating away in Leontes's consciousness. Most important of all, perhaps, they give us, the audience, a very rich sense of the dynamic between the characters. Listening to their light-hearted banter, while watching Leontes watching them, we gradually experience *his* growing, poisonous state of mind. Like someone picking at a sore, he continues to encourage her in the behaviour that is making him angry.

Hermione wins Polixenes over by being alive to his language and countering each of his points; he has said that he is afraid his absence will breed discontent at home, she says that they had news just yesterday that all in Bohemia is well (ll. 11–14, 30–2); he says their love in making him stay is a 'whip' to him, she, rather pointedly says that if only he had said he wanted to see his son they would let him go, and if he had *sworn* that that was what he wanted to do, they would 'thwack him hence with distaffs' – which is a wonderfully inappropriate image for a queen to use (ll. 25, 34–7). She ridicules him on his use of the mild oath 'verily' and, in offering him the choice of being her prisoner or her guest, draws attention to the speciousness of his argument about debt while echoing Leontes's use of the proverb about praise in departing: as her prisoner, he would pay a fee when he leaves and thus be able to save his thanks (ll. 54–5).

61–89 A chain of metaphors in Hermione's and Polixenes's language of friendship foreshadows the events that will result from Leontes's punishment of their supposed adultery: the words 'prisoner', 'offending', 'commit', 'punish', 'gaoler', 'Not guilty', mingle with words which in other contexts might have sexual overtones or connotations, 'potent', 'tricks', 'ill-doing', 'blood', 'playfellow', as well as the more explicitly sexual but still euphemistic 'By this we gather / You have tripp'd since' (I.ii.51–80).

Polixenes's account of his childhood games with Leontes (a golden age when time stood still and they thought to be 'Boy eternal') is suddenly ended by these 'temptations' of adulthood: they 'tripped', 'slipped' – there was a fall from that Garden of Eden. Hermione stops him lest he start to say that she and his (unnamed) queen 'are devils', and then manfully shoulders the woman's burden: the queens will answer their men's offences provided 'you first sinn'd with us, and that with us / You did continue fault, and that you slipp'd not / With any but with us' (ll. 86–8). These sexual overtones might encourage Leontes who is already suspicious of her behaviour to hear 'us' as the royal 'me'. But her clear-sighted, affectionate amusement at both her husband and his friend, her interest in their childhoods together, the presence of her son and her enquiry about Polixenes's young son combine to give an audience an impression of her strength and openness of character. She is her own woman and does not need an affair.

89–110 For Leontes, Hermione's success in getting Polixenes to stay merely highlights his own failure, which her playful (and entirely innocent) teasing of him and continued sexual banter do nothing to quell. Her extended verbal play on 'Grace' with its connotation of salvation is a nice counterpart to her previous language of 'fall'. But in his memory of their past together, her slight delay in accepting his suit, which in any other mind would be proof of her prudence and rectitude, now becomes suspiciously 'Three crabbed months' that 'soured themselves to death' before she would 'clap' hands with him in the binding but pre-marriage ceremony of handfasting (ll. 103–7). He perhaps suspects that she loved Polixenes even then.

Her teasing acceptance of his proposition that she has spoken to the purpose just twice calls out for her to give one hand to Leontes on the word 'husband' and the other to Polixenes on the word 'friend' (l. 110). There is no stage direction (SD) to that effect in the Folio but it has long been a stage tradition; editors usually add a SD, but only requiring her to give her hand to Polixenes. Either way, the word 'friend' is often a euphemism for 'lover', and to a jealous husband any such gesture might seem a travesty of that former handfasting.

110–121 By abandoning syntax almost altogether and relying instead simply on the rhythm and line length of blank verse to hold things together, Shakespeare is able to simulate Leontes's dangerously disturbed mental state. He is in a fever of jealousy, his mind skipping from one idea to another by association: they say … women say … [women] will say anything … women are as false as all the most false things in the world. At the same time, 'full like me' is echoed in the unspoken proverb 'full as an egg' which underlies the spoken proverb 'like as eggs' (ll. 131–2). His attention is torn between his son whom he loves, but whom he now doubts is his son, and his unhealthy obsession for his wife.

121–139 Leontes calls Mamillius to him and we are presented with the disturbing sight of him engaged in fatherly care, wiping the child's nose, while observing closely what he sees as the too-friendly gestures of his friend and his wife. He tries to talk genially to the child but his language is strewn with words which contain elements of sexual punning, beginning with the term of endearment 'bawcock' – ostensibly 'fine fellow' (l. 123). The image of innocent lambs, with which Polixenes had described their childhoods together (ll. 69–70), now becomes 'How now, you wanton calf, / Art thou my calf?' (I.ii.128–9),

punning on 'neat' in regard to the child's appearance and as another
word for bovine animal, as he himself notes (I.ii.125–7). The smutched /
neat nose has led naturally in his distorted imagination to the wanton calf. The nose, that pointed thruster-in which makes for a lewd
joke about husbands in *Antony and Cleopatra* (1.ii.54–7), is also commonly looked-for as a marker of family, inherited resemblance. He
not only wonders aloud whether the child is really his, he also asks
him directly. It is an unforgivable question for a parent to ask a child.
It is also an expression of his own mental anguish. A recent production showed Leontes as being quite violent towards Mamillius here,
making a modern point about family violence, but this is perhaps
too easy a solution, and detracts from the torture that Leontes is
exerting on *himself*. Leontes is undoubtedly the cause of the trauma
that is about to engulf his family, but he is not necessarily responsible
for it.

140–148 This play is showing us recognisable symptoms of mental
illness, even while describing them in terms of early modern ideas
of physiology. Leontes is in the grip of an 'affection', emotion, which
stabs at the core of his being – perhaps even to the extent of giving him
physical pain in his stomach, which he relates to Hermione's swollen
belly. His language breaks down further as he attempts to define both
his personal turmoil and the relationship between emotion and cog-
nition, which still evades full scientific explanation. His emotion is
'co-active' with the 'unreal' and 'fellow'st nothing'. It is *therefore* believable, 'credent', that it may 'co-join with something' (with its pun on
'thing' as female sexuality). If his affections can do this, so can hers
(ll. 140–4). In other words, his affection has no tangible basis, he does
not know why he feels this way and he cannot believe that Hermione
can be guilty, and yet he is convinced she is. We have seen how genuinely affectionate she is, and also, in that same word's other sense,
how passionate. Leontes's choice of language supplies a kind of logic
which 'proves' that she must be guilty. Sliding from one meaning
of a word to another, via rhetorical devices such as repetition and
antithesis, Shakespeare's poetry simulates Leontes's state of mind. In
turn that language convinces him of his suspicions. And of course,
emotion, even if groundless, is always felt in the body, and this gives
it a bodily reality: he can 'find it', feel it, in his 'hard'ning' brows, his
cuckold's horns (ll. 146–8). His logic is circular and self-fulfilling.

148–191 Hermione and Polixenes have noticed Leontes's disquiet, and approach him, expressing the affection of wife and friend, which he tries to deflect by asking Polixenes how he is. He then pretends that looking at his son he has been transported back to his own childhood. This repetition of the idea of father/son likeness is marked by yet another proverb about eggs (l. 163), this time, one about being fobbed off with things so cheap as to be worthless. Whereas Leontes's childhood dagger was 'muzzled', Mamillius says he will fight. This is a cocky response that may elicit indulgent smiles from the adults. Polixenes, who as Hermione has already pointed out, has not said that he needs to go home to see his own son, protests that he does indeed think the world of him. There is, however, something unsettling about his metaphors: the days seem short when they are home together – or does the child turn summer into winter (l. 170)? There is an underlying sense that both these men use their sons for their own purposes, a reversal of the caring role. Leontes now demonstrates this by saying that he and Mamillius will walk together, but his purpose is not to be with his son but to throw his friend and his wife together. In a continuation of the circular logic of the earlier speech (ll. 130–48), he is almost willing them to be unfaithful with each other in order to justify his suspicion. When she walks away taking Polixenes's arm and gazing directly into his face, he feels he is wading through proof of his cuckoldry, 'inch thick, knee deep' (ll. 184–7; see pp. 106–8). Although proverbially, one can be 'over head and ears' in anything, the phrase is most usually used of being in love. Here, over his head, he says, are his forked cuckold's horns. He tells Mamillius to go and play, but the child is perhaps confused by this change of plan and just stands there. Again, word association intensifies Leontes's sense of wrong: in telling Mamillius to 'go play', he thinks of the sexual foreplay that he believes Hermione is indulging in. This makes him think of the part that he believes he has been forced to play, that of cuckold, although we will interpret his play-acting as the deceitful subterfuge that we have just witnessed.

191–209 Ignoring the child, Leontes now briefly addresses us direct, perhaps even picking out individual men in the audience to suggest that their wives are having affairs. Audiences are often both thrilled and slightly embarrassed by such direct contact – even more so when the content of what is being said is so inherently embarrassing. They may laugh. In Greg Doran's production at Stratford, Anthony Sher enjoyed this, standing at the edge of the stage in urbane mood. Other actors might be more aggressive. The speech uses increasing amounts of alliteration; 's' and 'sh' combine to make a sloshy evocation of the sexual act; plosive 'b's and 'p's, and a revolted, sexual 'in and out' rhythm (l. 206) make a violent culmination. The poor and presumably terrified child tries to placate him by responding to the earlier question, 'I am like you' (l. 208), although the thought that he might be like someone behaving so oddly might be even more frightening.

209–237   Leontes calls Camillo, who has been standing observing the scene from a distance, and he dismisses Mamillius. Maybe the observation 'thou'rt an honest man' goes a little way to reassure the child and make him feel grown-up, but Leontes's reason for saying it is partly because he believes that Polixenes is *not* an honest man. Again, we might think that Mamillius is being made to bear too much of the burden of his parents' sexuality.

Leontes quite aggressively seems to suggest that Polixenes has decided to impose himself on their hospitality for longer (l. 212). Camillo retells exactly what we have all seen – that despite Leontes's entreaties, Polixenes kept (metaphorically) hauling in his anchor, ready to depart, and that it was Hermione who succeeded in persuading him to stay. Leontes interprets this as the court whispering scandal. His use of the word 'perceive' (l. 216) is important, both because his belief in Hermione's unfaithfulness is an erroneous interpretation of what he has seen, and because his way of describing what is happening (which is also the way he persuades himself of the validity of what he is seeing) is designed (by Shakespeare) to make us hear the associations in his words. Some of these associations may be intended by the character. Some may not be.

With bitter innuendo he proceeds to give a sexual connotation to everything Camillo now says. He knows that Camillo is intelligent, observant and discreet, as befits a careful and trusted adviser. To say that such a person soaks up information like a sponge is a fairly common simile. But to say that his 'conceit is soaking' (l. 224) places Camillo and his understanding within the disgusted evocation of the wetness of the sexual act noted at ll. 192–206. Leontes attacks him for pretending to be more intelligent and sensitive than the other servants. The word 'messes' here (l. 227), merely denotes the places where people eat according to rank, but transferred to denote the people themselves, it too carries a sense of disgust and also of a mixture of something sloppy. He seizes on Camillo's innocent use of the word 'satisfy' (ll. 234–6) as the final proof that he is complicit in Hermione's guilt.

237–269 Leontes's choice of the phrase 'chamber-counsels' (by which he means the private political advice given to a monarch by those advisers closest to him) then combines with the arresting, intimate, image that Camillo has performed a 'priest-like' duty in cleansing his 'bosom' (his feelings, heart). Together these words raise the question of 'sin' in the context of body and bedchamber, while even suggesting that Camillo has been counselling him on his own sexual perform-ance. Finally he directly accuses Camillo of being dishonest, or if not that, a coward, negligent, or a fool. Camillo responds in careful, measured terms, admitting that we can all be 'negligent, foolish and fearful' from time to time, but that he has never wilfully betrayed Leontes's trust (ll. 244–69).

269–286 Leontes continues to ask whether Camillo has not seen, heard and therefore thought, that Hermione is a whore, insisting on the answer 'yes': if Camillo has not seen it, it must be because his scholar's glasses are thicker than they would be if they were made not of glass but of cuckolds' horn. This echoes the earlier ideas that all men are cuckolds and that the cuckold is the last to know about his wife's infidelity (ll. 192–201, 218–19). Denial of this would, he says, constitute 'impudence', a rejection of authority.

Camillo here demonstrates his absolute worth as a counsellor. He does not tell Leontes outright that he is wrong since he would not be believed. Instead he protests that the accusation does not become Leontes and states quite vehemently that he will not stand by to hear Hermione accused thus without taking action. His loyalty is as much to her, his mistress, as to the king, and he can rightly defend her sim-ply on those terms. His language echoes the earlier part of the scene. Whereas Leontes had previously told Hermione 'thou never spok'st to better purpose' (l. 90), Camillo now tells him 'You never spoke what did become you less'. Hermione spoke 'grace' twice. He says that were Leontes to speak again in the same terms it would be 'sin' as bad as the actual, 'true', act of which he is accusing her. Since it is not possible to prove innocence (which is why justice depends on proving guilt), his language has to allow for the possibility of her adultery. He therefore attacks the accusation itself, rather than its substance: reiteration of the accusation would be as sinful as that act would be if it had actually happened, even though the accusation would now be true.

286–300 The listing of all the little gestures of lovemaking is made more evocative by the repeated combination of body parts ('cheek', 'noses', 'lip') with verbs in their participle form ('leaning', 'meeting', 'kissing') suggesting continuous, never ending action. It is the enraged, jealous rantings of someone who imagines that the people around him are at it like rabbits. Again, there is an instance of the distortion of time, 'Wishing clocks more swift' (ll. 291–2). But the repeated 'ing' sound leads inexorably to 'nothing', again with it's pun on 'thing' as female sexual organ. Philosophically, and in physics, nothing can come of nothing. A version of that truth marked King Lear's incipient madness (see *Tragedy of King Lear* 1.i.90). Leontes simply asserts that this nothing is a something, because otherwise all things would be nothing. It is, if anything, more mad, more nihilistic, than the earlier tragedy. The repeated references to blindness here likewise recall the actual and the metaphorical blindness of characters in *Lear*. Camillo now gives up on counsel and turns to flat denial ('No, no, my lord'), but realises that remonstrance is useless – and also dangerous to him. Like Othello, Leontes's jealousy, imagining all those little acts of adultery, has now created for itself the 'ocular proof' (*Othello*, III.iii.365).

300–308 The words 'infect' and its derivatives (infection, infectious, infected) are not especially common in Shakespeare, but there are six occurrences in the course of this scene (ll. 147, 264, 307, 308, 418, 423). The run of these images in this section began with Camillo's suggestion that Leontes's fear of Hermione's loyalty infects his wisdom (l. 264), plus his reference to Leontes's 'diseased opinion' (l. 299). But Leontes now angrily refutes this suggestion of his own sickness by applying the word to his wife (l. 307). The multiple senses of the word at this period are relevant. Primarily, of course, it signifies the spread of disease, particularly through air or water. But it also means to spoil, corrupt, or adulterate; to taint with moral corruption; to affect someone with emotion; and to imbue with a strong opinion or belief.

As something in the air, the word associates readily with 'nostril' and smell or 'savour' (l. 421), and also with the influence of the stars (ll. 201–3, 425–31). The word, and the same idea expressed in other words, spreads like an infection through the entire scene. It will recur in Hermione's speech at her trial when she observes that she is being treated as one infectious to her children (III.ii.96–7), and again near the end of the play when at last Leontes will hope that 'the blessed gods will purge infection from the air' (V.i.169).

309–310 Leontes thinks of his erstwhile friend as having won Hermione, wearing her like a trophy, a medal hanging round his neck (ll. 309–10). Perhaps Polixenes is indeed wearing such a medal, one that bears her image, and which she must have given him. Rulers and aristocrats commonly gave such medals as marks of gracious condescension to courtiers or visitors, and as symbols of their power, or celebrations of a particular event. This normal part of Renaissance social currency and courtly interaction becomes in his imagination a secret yet also blatant expression of their supposed adultery.

310–364 When Leontes demands that Camillo should 'bespice' or infect (l. 318) Polixenes's drinking cup, Camillo's only course of action is to pretend to agree. He claims that he is indeed capable of the act (ll. 322–3), but still tries to defend Hermione. He uses the word 'crack' in the sense of 'flaw' but the word carries a sexual pun on slit or rather 'vulva', an association which perhaps prompts the next angry outburst from his master. Leontes, demands whether it is likely that he should have corrupted, sullied and spotted his own sense of peace by accusing Hermione falsely (ll. 326–35). Camillo can only pretend to believe him, although he urges him to seem friendly towards Polixenes. Left on stage alone, however, he makes it clear to us that he has no intention of becoming a murderer, and that whether he kills Polixenes or not, he knows his own life is in danger.

364–376 Polixenes now enters. He is surprised and puzzled because Leontes has just swept past him, refusing to look at him or return his greeting, as if he had just lost the possession of an entire province, or a 'region / Loved as he loves himself'. The image unwittingly both recalls the biblical injunction that a husband should love his wife as his own flesh (St Paul, Ephesians 5.25–30) and Leontes's comparison of an adulterous wife to a walled town that lets 'in and out' the enemy (l. 197). It may even, to some in the audience, recall King James I's claim in his first speech to the English Parliament that he was like a husband to the kingdom of England.

377–431 Polixenes, who had begun his part in the play with courtly elliptical speech, now demands that Camillo speak the direct truth. He observes Camillo's changed complexion, and says he feels as alarmed as Camillo looks (ll. 380–4). But rather than answering him immediately, Camillo picks up on the language of infection: 'There is a sickness ... caught / Of you, that yet are well' (ll. 384–7). Eventually, Camillo brings himself to tell Polixenes the shocking news that he has been commissioned to murder him (l. 412), and then of the accusation of adultery with Hermione. This is even more shocking to him and makes him feel as if he is indeed infected, a Judas, a pariah (ll. 416–24).

432 to the end At last, after four hundred lines of surmise, suspicion, evasion, and language that slides from one meaning to another, there is brisk urgency in the plan that follows. Camillo will arrange for Polixenes's followers to slip quietly out of the city. He is adamant that there is no time to lose. He is offering his services to Polixenes, but will not wait while Polixenes tries to check out the truth of his story (ll. 439–44).

Polixenes states that his ships are ready at anchor since he had intended to leave two days before. But any responsibility he may have towards Hermione's future safety is slid over in the kind of line and sentence construction that has been a hallmark of this scene: 'Good expedition be my friend, and comfort / The gracious Queen' (l. 458). The primary grammatical meaning is 'May speed be a friend to me and comfort a friend to the Queen' although the wish is rather vacuous. Any interpretation more aware of Hermione's equally desperate situation requires some stretching of the grammar, as in 'May the speed of my departure both help me and bring comfort to the queen (in removing the source of Leontes's anger)'. A very slight pause marking the end of the poetic line, however, would momentarily let us hear the entirely selfish 'Speed be my friend and comfort'. Polixenes's flight will confirm Hermione's guilt in Leontes's mind. Shakespeare's management of Polixenes's language here suggests that he does not want him to get off entirely blame-free in our minds.

ACT II

Act II, scene i

1–34   The scene is in marked contrast to the previous one. The characters on stage – Hermione, her son and ladies – immediately indicate a domestic scene. Since Mamillius is still in their care, he must be 'unbreeched', i.e. in the long skirts that male children wore until they were seven. Many productions show a nursery setting with toys, but it could equally be the queen's private apartment – as it is in the source. She and Mamillius have been talking or playing together, but either the late stages of pregnancy are getting to her or the child is being particularly tiresome. Either way, she needs a short break.

Mamillius is a rather more challenging little boy in this scene than he was in the previous one with his father. Like most children his age, he does not want to be treated like a baby, but he is perhaps precocious in his chat with the ladies about women's eyebrows. The first textual mention of Hermione's pregnancy is not until line 18, but the First Lady's next comment seems calculated to tease the child into jealousy for his unborn sibling (ll. 16–19). This scene too thus has a disturbing undertone of sexuality and jealousy. Hermione, however, has a delightful and affectionate relationship with her son. She takes him seriously, inviting him to tell her a story, offering him the choice as to what kind it should be, and agreeing to his preference for a 'sad' tale as being more suitable for winter. Mamillius's choice of the kind of scary fairy tale in which most children delight now defines 'winter's tale' for us: not the proverbial definition, a long drawn-out story suitable for a long drawn-out winter's night, but something altogether more frightening, which begins in a churchyard. As in the very first scene, he is connected with death (see I.i.35–46). Hermione plays along, wanting to be pretend-frightened too, and invites him to whisper the story in her ear.

34.1–57   The storytelling continues in silence, although there might well be gestures of mock spookiness and fear as Mamillius acts out his tale and Hermione listens. Leontes, Antigonus and other lords enter and talk at the back of the stage. Camillo's scheme regarding his escape with Polixenes has gone exactly according to the plan we heard earlier, but this has only confirmed Leontes's suspicions. Camillo has undeniably betrayed Leontes by refusing to poison Polixenes as he had promised. Leontes now assumes that Camillo must have been Polixenes's 'pander', the person who arranged the adultery. He claims that his previous suspicions, the things he 'mistrusted', are proved true, and that this firm knowledge is now poisoning him. As so often in this play, however, the audience can hear the opposite meaning in the words: we know that Leontes's mind was poisoned previously, and that the things and people he 'mistrusted' are actually 'true' (in the sense of 'loyal') to him (l. 50).

58–97 The two different moods that have been presented side by side on stage now clash violently. Leontes angrily seizes the child, though Hermione at first assumes that this is some other game. She firsts defends herself in the conditional tense – this is what I would say if you were accusing me for real, and you would believe me (ll. 64–6). Leontes ignores her and proceeds to point her out to the bystanders as if she were an object. Again, his accusation slides on a double meaning: 'honourable' (l. 70) can mean both honest and of high status, but he chooses to take it purely in the latter sense. Playacting also enters into this attack as he corrects his choice of the word 'calumny'. But in fact the entire speech is a demonstration of calumnious insinuation; it takes thirteen lines before he comes out with the unambiguous accusation of adultery (ll. 66–80).

Her denial is dignified. She does not accuse Leontes of villainy, merely of making a mistake. But Leontes, who throughout has seemed very conscious of status, perhaps hears 'villain' as 'villein' (low-born peasant). He calls her 'thing' rather than 'queen', insisting on the distinction of his status as king and therefore sliding into accusing her not just of adultery but of treason (l. 91). The only title to which he thinks she is now entitled is (presumably) that of 'whore' (ll. 95–7).

97–127 Characteristically, Hermione's next speech focuses on others: Camillo is not part of any plot (partly of course because no such plot existed); and Leontes, once he reflects on the truth, will be grieved that he made these accusations. When that happens, however, his mere apology for making a mistake will scarcely be sufficient. As previously, Leontes feels that if he is wrong, the earth itself would disappear to nothing (I.ii.295–8). He admits no denial and anyone who defends Hermione will be accounted a traitor.

Although Leontes orders his followers to take Hermione to prison, they do not move. Instead, Hermione addresses them. She is perfectly calm, and indeed observes that her lack of womanish tears may perhaps incline them to disbelieve her. Instead she picks up on Leontes's term 'honourable' – an honourable grief that burns at the dishonour done both to her status and to her reputation, and which is therefore honourable for her to hold. Leontes's half line 'Shall I be heard?' (l. 117) is both an expression of impotence in the face of her calm eloquence, and an angry observation that no one has yet obeyed his previous command. Hermione saves the embarrassment of the courtiers by taking command of the situation herself, organising which of her women is to go with her, pointedly asking for confirmation from Leontes that that will be allowed, and gesturing to her pregnant belly, 'My plight requires it' (l. 120). She tells the ladies not to cry, and leads the way to prison. Using the word 'grace' for the third time (see I.ii.101, 107), she embraces her imprisonment as an expression, and an honourable trial, of both her social status and her state of moral grace. The stage direction that is traditionally added here by editors that she exits 'guarded' seems superfluous, and she might even leave the stage before the confused and reluctant gentlemen have made a move.

128–59 Leontes's followers urge him to reconsider, knowingly risking imprisonment or worse themselves by contradicting him. Antigonus's line about turning his wife's lodging into a stable if Hermione is guilty is so startling that it often attracts a laugh. But the evocation of the dirt and smell of a stables would allow him a facial expression of disgust, which in turn allows us to hear a sexual pun on 'ride'. The idea of not trusting his wife further than he could see her and feel her, elicits the metaphor of hunting dogs coupled together on a single leash, but in the context also allows us to hear a sexual pun on 'couple' (ll. 136–7). There may also be a specific topical allusion (see pp. 108–9). Ironically, this defence of Hermione takes the same intellectual and grammatical construction as Leontes's accusation of her at I.ii.295–8. Antigonus's desperate conclusion, however, is more outrageous than anything that Leontes has yet devised: were Hermione to be guilty, all women would be guilty and he would 'geld' or sterilise his three young daughters (ll. 145–52). He thus lives up to the meaning of his Greek name, 'against child bearing'. Clearly Antigonus means to dissuade Leontes from his course of action. But Leontes will hear no dissent and instead expresses resentment at what he sees as involvement in his own private grievance: he sees and feels what Antigonus refuses to see and could not feel. Leontes must here exert some physical pain on Antigonus with his hands – 'the instruments that feel' – perhaps grabbing and twisting his hair, ear or indeed 'nose' (ll. 153–6). The image of the stables has one final echo in 'dungy earth' (l. 159).

159 to the end   Leontes appeals to the other lords to believe him, but when the lord refuses, he falls back on his kingship; his right to rule ('prerogative') does not need counsel, and as king he has a 'natural goodness' and understanding of the truth. As both king and husband the affair is his and his alone. In a very barbed comment, Antigonus wishes that he had kept it private and not made an 'overture' (opening) of it to the world (l. 174). Leontes dismisses this with scorn: the circumstantial evidence, including Camillo's flight, is so strong it lacks only the visual proof of seeing them in the act. But in order to forestall public censure, he has sent two trusted servants, Cleomenes and Dion, to the oracle at Delphos. Despite his previous claim to supreme power, he again asks for confirmation that he is acting correctly, displaying a corner of self-doubt–although he cannot see it, which is a recognisable symptom of his mental state. The Lord gives him the approbation he desires, but Antigonus is alienated. The situation remains desperate but Antigonus is the first person to suggest the possibility that this story could raise laughter (l. 200). As yet it is the terrible laughter that comes with horror (see pp. 95–6).

Act II, scene ii

0.1–4   The indeterminate setting of the public theatre stages, with little scenery beyond indicative props like a table, throne, or bed meant that a scene could switch instantaneously, indicated purely by the identity of the characters on stage and their dialogue. The public theatres had at least two doors, one on either side of the stage, and probably a central door as well, as shown in the famous 'de Witt' drawing of the Swan theatre. Paulina, whom we have not met before, enters from one of the side doors with 'a Gentleman and attendants' and asks the Gentleman to go and fetch the Keeper of the prison. As will be made clear at l. 15, the attendants are her servants. Most editors treat the Gentleman too as if he had come with Paulina, but, as will also become clearer, the scene is conceived as one of the outer rooms of the prison and it therefore makes more sense for the Gentleman to be one of the prison officers. He exits by the opposite door, conceived as leading to the inner parts of the building. We can imagine that while she is waiting, Paulina walks round the stage, looking about her at this unaccustomed building, while commenting on how unsuitable a place it is for Hermione. The fact that this remark is prefaced by an address to the absent Hermione as 'Good Lady' indicates that she is talking to herself and not addressing the audience directly.

4–23   The Gentleman returns with the prison keeper, now referred to in the SDs as 'Jailer'. She first checks that the Jailer recognises her. She is perhaps stressing her rank, but perhaps more importantly doing everything openly, by the book. As yet, the audience does not know who she is, except that she is a friend or supporter of Hermione, although her manner of dress and commanding air will also indicate her rank and perhaps her character. The Jailer replies that he knows her to be a 'worthy' lady and respects her (ll. 5–6). She asks to see Hermione but he says that he has already been ordered not to allow this. She belittles this with her homely but dismissive 'Here's ado' (l. 10), and then asks to see one of Hermione's women. The three questions here as she homes in on one of the women by name, plus her use of the word 'lawful' suggests both that she is feeling her way round the previous prohibition, and also that the Jailer is having to think on his feet, since he does not at first reply (ll. 12–13). His orders did not extend to the waiting women and he does not know whether he should include them. A pause between each question would help to convey the tension here. The Jailer finally acquiesces, on condition that her attendants withdraw. She agrees to this and her attendants leave by the door by which they entered.

There are no exits marked here in Folio; all were first supplied by the play's earliest editors. If the Gentleman is her companion, he leaves with the attendants – which is the stage direction in most editions. If he is one of the prison staff, he might usher the attendants out and then wait at the door. In that case, the Jailer could motion to him to go back 'inside' the prison to fetch Emilia. The Jailer stipulates that he must be present throughout the meeting. Paulina agrees, but not without some impatience at the restrictions. In most editions, the Jailer exits here to fetch Emilia, but if the Gentleman has already gone to do this, her comment (using the word 'ado' again) is said deliberately and provocatively in his earshot, if not directly to him (ll. 22–3). This might add to his embarrassment at what he is being compelled to do, and is in character with her behaviour towards Leontes himself in the following scene. She observes that these excessive restrictions, treating spotless Hermione as if she were a dangerous criminal, create an indelible stain – such as cannot be obliterated with dye. She was not present in Act I scene ii to hear Leontes's angry simile there about falsehood in women (I.ii.132–5), but her comment echoes and reverses his.

23 to the end   Emilia enters and tells her that because of the emotional disruption of the last few days, Hermione has given birth slightly early. Paulina's eager question that the child is a boy may be because she is already planning on how to use it to get through to Leontes; he might be more receptive to another heir. The repeated insistence through the scene that the little girl is completely innocent, and that Hermione is as innocent as she, is in marked contrast to Leontes's assertion that all women are equally false, or Antigonus's wild claim that if Hermione is false then all women are so – and he will 'geld' his own daughters. Antigonus is Paulina's husband, although the text has not yet identified her as such, and an audience will not yet be aware of it.

Paulina suggests that she should take the child to show the king in the hope of softening his heart. She reassures Emilia that she will tell Leontes the absolute truth; if she does not, she hopes proverbially that her tongue will 'blister'. Ironically, of course, as she has already demonstrated, and as she wryly admits (ll. 37–8), she does in fact have a blistering tongue, in the sense that she does not suffer fools or injustice silently. Emilia readily agrees to the scheme because Hermione has been considering just such a plan, but had dared not ask anyone for fear of being denied (ll. 50–4). With great relief, Emilia invites Paulina to come and see Hermione but the Jailer intervenes. He now states that he has no authority to let the baby out of prison. Paulina resorts to formal, legalistic language to reassure him that the child was born free from any guilt and that it is therefore not legal to incarcerate it. She promises to defend him against any accusation of wrongdoing.

Act II, scene iii

0.1–26　Again, F's composite stage direction lists Antigonus, Paulina and servants with Leontes at the beginning, but Leontes should come on stage alone. He cannot sleep for thinking about Hermione's supposed adultery. A servant enters and tells him that Mamillius has had a good night; we thereby learn that it is early morning and that the child is sick. Needless to say, Leontes attributes the boy's illness too to distress at his mother's guilt. He dismisses the servant. With reasons taken from the source, *Pandosto*, Leontes is angry with himself for not being able to take revenge on Polixenes, who has too many powerful allies. He feels Polixenes and Camillo laughing at him, which of course increases his anger towards Hermione.

26.1–42　There is a commotion at the door. Antigonus, Lords and Servants are trying to bar Paulina's way. They enter but remain near the door at the back of the stage. She is carrying the baby. Male–female relations are brought into sharp focus throughout this scene. She appeals to the men, the 'lords', to fulfil their chivalric duty and support ('second') her in her fight for the queen's life, asking them if they are afraid of the king's tyranny (ll. 27–9). She says that Hermione is more 'free' than he is 'jealous' (l. 30). The word 'free' encapsulates the problem. Leontes is accusing Hermione of being too free with her favours, but Paulina is using the word in two other senses: both 'innocent' and 'honourable'. Antigonus tries to shut her up with the informal 'That's enough' (l. 30), while the servant explains that Leontes has not slept. She retorts that their pussyfooting support of his behaviour is making things worse. A lawyer in the previous scene, she is now a doctor, promising to purge the physical imbalance that is causing his sleeplessness. Leontes complains about the disturbance and Paulina calls out that it is not noise but necessary conversation about 'gossips' (l. 41). She is indeed 'audacious', both in contradicting him and potentially, in her reference to 'gossips', for although that word could signify godparents of either sex, it also meant those women attending a woman during her lying-in. There is a domesticity and femininity about the word that Leontes, in his present state of mind, finds insufferable.

42–52　Now for the first time we learn that Paulina is Antigonus's wife – hence the terse familiarity of his command at l. 30. Leontes, it seems, knew that Paulina would visit him and has previously ordered Antigonus to prevent this. When Antigonus protests that he has tried, Leontes scornfully asks 'Can'st not rule her?' (l. 46). We are into the age-old debate about mastery in marriage, now linked to the equally old problem of what to do when ordered to carry out an immoral act. We have seen Hermione living up to the renaissance ideal of 'companionate' marriage, in which man and wife as one flesh work together for a common goal. Now, Paulina jumps in to answer the question addressed to her husband: he may rule her against being dishonest but he cannot stop her 'committing' honesty (i.e. being honest against orders) unless he were to commit her (to prison, as Leontes has done to Hermione). This verbal dexterity seems to exhaust Antigonus – probably not for the first time. In a return to the horse metaphors he used at II.i.136–50, he explains that when she gets the bit between her teeth like this, there is nothing for it but to give her her head, but he recognises that 'she'll not stumble' (ll. 50–2), i.e. she does not need his control because she is usually right. The control of a horse is commonly used at this period as an image for the control of the passions.

52–74   By addressing Leontes now as 'my liege', Paulina stresses that her behaviour springs from her deep sense of loyalty to him. She states that in daring to appear antagonistic she is actually a more loyal servant, doctor and adviser than those who are encouraging him in his 'evils' by going along with them. Her use of the phrase 'good queen' brings an exasperated exclamation from Leontes and when she insists on repeating it, even shouting him down, there need to be sharp intakes of breath and other small gestures of alarm from the men standing around, something in short to attract her attention, because she turns on them, intensifying the point she made previously at l. 27: if she were a man, even the worst, the lowliest and least honourable among them, she would undertake a trial by combat to prove Hermione's innocence. Leontes orders the men to manhandle her out of the chamber; she stands her ground, one hand raised (she still has the baby in the other arm), threatening to scratch the eyes out of the first man who touches her (l. 63). Momentarily, the image is almost that of a bear being baited. She says she will go of her own accord, but only after she has done what she has come to do. Repeating the word 'good' twice more, she now presents Leontes with his baby daughter, completing the traditional role of the midwife in showing the baby to the waiting father. Leontes, however, is outraged by what he sees as her impropriety: she is too mannish to be a proper woman and as a go-between between his estranged queen and himself, she is continuing her activity as the bawd who must have relayed secret messages (intelligence) between the queen and Polixenes. Paulina jumps in, turning his words back on him: she is as honest as he is mad (and if she seems mad herself in the way she is behaving, that is enough to pass for honesty, for the world is so corrupt that it is madness to be honest). Again he orders his followers to remove her but they are transfixed.

74–93   With the baby lying on the floor, the focus of the next part of the scene is on Antigonus and his role as a husband. Leontes tries to make him pick it up and give it back to Paulina by impugning his manhood: he is unroosted (l. 75, 'knocked off his perch', perhaps also *unroostered*, 'castrated'). She, with equal force tells her husband that if he touches it his hands will be forever 'unvenerable' (l. 78, dishonoured, but unwittingly carrying the warning that they will never grow old). Leontes points out the still motionless Antigonus with the scoff, 'He dreads his wife' (l. 80), but again Paulina turns the tables on him: if Leontes were to 'dread' (respect) his wife he would acknowledge his own children.

Leontes now accuses them both of colluding: 'a nest of traitors' (l. 82). Again, Paulina turns his words back, this time electing to speak for everyone on stage: no one is a traitor except Leontes. He alone has betrayed the entire royal family to slander, and obstinately he will not remove the rotten root of this opinion. But the careful lawyer of the previous scene has given way to passion. Paulina has effectively been reduced to trading insults. And because the case against Hermione is one entirely of opinion, her method of proving Hermione's innocence is rhetorically almost identical with Leontes's method of proving her guilt. Her use of opposites as comparison, 'I am as ignorant in that as you / In so entitling me, and no less honest / Than you are mad' (70–2), 'The root of his opinion, which is rotten / As ever oak or stone was sound' (ll. 90–1), both hark back structurally to 'were they false / As o'erdyed blacks … yet were it true' (I.ii.133–6). Still harping on her supposed degeneracy and her mastery over her husband, it is now Leontes's turn to recall the animal-baiting image (l. 93).

93–114   The presence of the nearly silent lords is an important part of the dynamics of the scene visually because, as we have already noted, it encourages the speaking characters to point things out. Paulina invites them to compare the baby's features with those of its father's. It is now her turn to make a gender reversal but this time the effect is more clearly risible. She hopes that Nature will ensure that the child's mind is different, with no hint of jealousy in it so that she does not grow up to doubt the paternity of her children (ll. 104–8). Women normally know the identity of their child's father. For Leontes to doubt he is the father of his own child is just as ludicrous. The nature of the argument between them means that it is not capable of being won, but she has clearly beaten Leontes at his own game. He is reduced to simple abuse, while Antigonus (as twice before) comments resignedly and humorously on the impossibility of controlling one's wife. Leontes, impotently, again orders her removal from the room and again threatens her with burning.

115–130   It is perhaps at this point that Paulina slips up. In stating that she will not call him a tyrant, she does of course do just that (l. 116). The rhetorical term is 'paralipsis' – the reference to a thing by pretending to dismiss it. Despite his threats, Leontes is justly able to point out that she is still alive and were he a tyrant she would be dead, although it might be more accurate to say that it is his lords who have so far saved his rule from tyranny by refusing to jump to his bidding. But this exchange breaks the spell on the courtiers and they at last start to remove Paulina from the chamber. She twice tells them not to push or manhandle her. Her parting shot is to accuse them again of serving the king badly because they listen to his 'follies' (l. 128). She might single out Antigonus for the phrase 'not one of you', and a refusal on his part to take her side, or even to meet her eye, would prompt the comment 'So, so.' In this case, 'Farewell, we are gone' would signify the end of her marriage as well as her exit from the stage (ll. 129–30). But presumably she does not really believe that Leontes is a tyrant or she would not leave the baby with him.

The scene makes a salutary political point. It takes more than just a cruel ruler to make a tyranny. Those who obey tyrannous commands, or simply turn a blind eye to the small incremental steps by which tyranny so often establishes itself, are also responsible. This political lesson is apparent in Shakespeare's earliest plays, underpinning the three parts of *Henry VI*, and made explicit in the role of the scrivener in *Richard III* (III.vi).

131–183 Leontes now exhibits the behaviour of a tyrant indeed, holding someone else responsible for the actions of a family member, and identifying a 'weakness' – Antigonus's sympathy for the child. He seeks to bind Antigonus to him by making him complicit in his own illegal and tyrannous act, the murder of the baby (ll. 131–42). The men now seek to appease Leontes. They reassure him that Antigonus was not responsible for his wife's action, and kneel (l. 149) to beg him to change his mind about killing the baby. But they beg it not as a matter of right and wrong but in recompense for their service past and to come, and for fear of what else might ensue. Such a request made in such circumstances is a hostage to fortune for it enables Leontes to grant what they ask and then, since they have nothing left with which to bargain, to demand something as bad, if not worse. But even so, Leontes is not going to be caught twice. He first exacts an oath from Antigonus that he will do anything to save the baby's life: a simple statement is not enough; he makes Antigonus swear on his sword. He then gives the order for the baby's exposure.

184–193 Antigonus picks up the baby, invoking supernatural powers in his hope that wild animals will care for it – as 'they say' can sometimes happen (ll. 186–9). He wishes Leontes better fortune than he deserves for this deed, and again wishes the baby blessing (ll. 189–91). Folio marks an exit for him at this point, so that Leontes's excuse that he will not rear another man's child is said, perhaps defensively, to those remaining on stage. There is, of course, a world of difference between refusing to rear a child and actively seeking its demise. As we have noted before, he seems to need approval.

193 to the end A servant enters with news that Cleomenes and Dion have returned in remarkably short time from the Delphic oracle and are on their way to the court. Leontes interprets the speed as indicative that the oracle will reveal the truth, and orders preparations for a trial of his 'disloyal' queen. It is clear that he has prejudged the outcome. He intends to execute her (ll. 205–6). He tells his lords to leave him and to make sure they follow his orders. But since the stage has to be cleared for the next scene, he will exit by one door, and the lords and servant by the other.

ACT III

Act III, scene i

1 to the end   Although they have landed in Sicily, Cleomenes and Dion are still travelling post haste back to the court. They may have baggage with them, and they are certainly carrying the precious, sealed oracle, although this may not be visible here. They are in the process of changing horses, but also in the middle of preparing for their appearance before the king, rehearsing what they will say about the countryside and temple at Delphos. But they also seem genuinely struck by the beauty of the place, the solemnity of the temple rituals, and the awesome, humbling experience of the oracle itself with its thunderous voice. They remark on how swift and easy their journey has been and, like Leontes in the previous scene, hope that this presages a clear outcome, but they are worried by the proclamations against the queen. There is a sense of racing against time, the 'violent carriage' – the hasty preparations for the trial, and perhaps the speed of their own journey – will, however, end it one way or another, and they are confident that when the oracle is opened, some extraordinary, 'rare', explanation will swiftly become apparent. Shakespeare gives Dion an unconscious pun on 'issue', child (l. 22), and since we are aware that we are only a third of the way through the play, we may well suspect there will be complications.

Act III, scene ii

1–9   We have reached the highpoint of the first half of the play, which has been anticipated and longed for by several different sets of characters. The intrinsic theatricality of a trial, its rituals, confrontations, and emotions, of course make it a popular setting for film and TV drama. On the bare early modern public stage, there would have been no major scene change for this scene (in contrast with Kean's nineteenth-century production, see pp. 134–6) but a throne for Leontes may have been pushed out through the centre doors. Since this scene does not start with characters already in the middle of a conversation as they walk on, which is the way Shakespeare commonly gets his characters on and off stage, it probably begins with a formal procession involving Leontes, his lords, and the officers of the court. One of them carries a large and imposing sword, since at l. 123 an officer refers to 'this sword of justice'. There might therefore also be a table in front of Leontes's throne on which it could be positioned (like the mace in the House of Commons) to indicate that the court is in session.

Leontes, as the judge of the court, opens the proceedings with a short, formal, public address, in which he again feels the necessity of absolving himself from the charge of tyranny. Since, however, he is also taking the roles of prosecutor and plaintiff, justice is unlikely. He orders the 'prisoner' to be brought forth, and this command is formally repeated, probably in full voice and perhaps with some ceremonial gesture, by the officer of the court.

9.1–11 Folio includes '*Hermione (as to her trial) Ladies*' as part of the block stage direction at the head of the scene, but marked off by colons (cf. pp. 1–2) to indicate a separate, later, entrance for her. This too is a procession, with the ladies who have been attending her in prison, and given the phrase 'as to her trial', presumably also involving officers as guards. It will therefore take time. In most modern editions and productions (following Nicholas Rowe), the Officer is also given the word 'Silence', but in the Folio, this word is printed in italics, and ranged to the right of the line, separated from the rest of his speech by a space of approximately 1 cm. It is probably not a piece of the dialogue, but a stage direction.

Shakespeare's texts are only sparsely supplied with explicit stage directions. Instead, necessary moves, indications of emotion, and other directions are made apparent in the dialogue. This may be because as an actor, Shakespeare had found that word and gesture reinforce each other in the memory, or because, as a writer, he wanted to exert a measure of directorial control. Short pauses, and the pace of delivery can often be suggested by altering the line length, or by choice of rhetorical structures. But the only way to ensure an extended silence is to supply a stage direction (see *Coriolanus*, V.iii.183 which orders a silence that can successfully be held for twenty or thirty seconds – an age in theatrical terms).

A spoken order of 'Silence' to quell a buzz of stage babble as Hermione comes into view is of course an obvious way of playing the scene, but it is something of a cliché, and might even create an air of salaciousness – a sense of people gathered to see what the adulterous queen looks like, or what she looks like now after childbirth. This is a

play which is very much about speech, ways of speaking and freedom
to speak, as Hermione's own speech in defence is about to make clear.
Few of the characters have been able openly and freely to express their
shock at the way she is being treated, although none has gone along
with it willingly. With the exception of Paulina, their reluctance to
obey orders has been largely mute, an expression of powerlessness,
fear, and passive rather than active resistance. Absolute silence as
she walks on would continue that pattern, afford her the dignity she
deserves, and also allow the audience the time and space to reflect.
(See pp. 102–3 and V.iii.21–42 below.)

12–53   The indictment now includes one further count against
Hermione: that she did advise Polixenes and Camillo to 'fly away by night'
(ll. 19–20). Hermione begins her defence by stating that no defence
is possible since all she can do is deny the accusation; she can offer
no proof. She turns to Leontes. In doing so, she might glance round
the whole court, inviting us to agree that everyone except Leontes
knows she is innocent. We, the offstage audience, are also included
in that, for she goes on to make the kind of meta-theatrical statement
in which Shakespeare delights: there can be no story, not even one
designed to please spectators (in a theatre) that presents a more innocent person (ll. 35–6).
    She points out the various aspects of royalty that she represents;
she is not only the king's bedfellow but his jointress or partner who
owns a right to the throne, the daughter of a king, and mother to a
future king. But having displayed herself in this magnificence, she
deplores the fact that she has to 'prate' about honour in front of people
like us who have chosen to come and hear her. Again she addresses
Leontes directly, appealing to his conscience, asking him to remember
how he used to feel about her, and how much she merited that. Again,
encompassing the whole audience, onstage and off, she hopes that
all who hear her will harden their hearts against her if she has ever
strayed 'one jot' outside the bounds of honour.
    If Leontes is seated in a throne in the centre back portion of the
stage, she will be positioned perhaps in one of the front corners, facing
him. It is a powerful place to be, close to the audience, and enables an
actor to take in the entire auditorium with the slightest turns of the
head. At the Globe in 1997, however, she was brought in from prison
in filthy, bloody clothes, as if she had given birth without the aid of

the ladies in prison with her (or had else been tortured), and was then enclosed in a cage in the centre of the stage, furthest from the audience (cf. p. 144). In being asked to act such an interpretation, the actor was compelled to mumble these powerful words. As a piece of theatre direction, it matched Leontes for misogyny.

53–75 Hermione's earlier misgivings are born out by Leontes's reaction to her speech, but his tortuous syntax demonstrates that it is not just that he does not believe her, but that he refuses to do so. His speech uses three negatives ('ne'er', 'wanted' i.e. lacked, 'Less'), combined with features that we have noted before: an appeal to old stories or popular opinion; and the use of complex comparisons. It demands to be spoken in a hectoring, aggressive tone. Again, because the whole case against her consists of assertion and commonplace supposition, the statement cannot be effectively denied. All she can do is state that it does not apply to her. Inevitably, Leontes reposts that she is merely not admitting her guilt (l. 58). She replies coolly that she must not admit to any faults other than those she is 'mistress of' (i.e. her own), and proceeds to go through each element in the case against her. She asserts that she knows not the 'taste' of conspiracy and will refuse to partake in it. We might remember Camillo's refusal to serve Polixenes with a poisoned cup, and Emilia telling Paulina that although she had talked about involving someone else to take the baby to Leontes, she felt unable to initiate such a plan (II.i.51–4).

76–90 Leontes of course knows that he had ordered Camillo to poison Polixenes. As is often the case with someone who has something to hide, he seeks to find a similar kind of fault in someone else, and without actually saying so, accuses her of wanting to murder him: 'you know / What you have underta'en to do in's absence' (ll. 76–7). The charges against her are multiplying. Hermione has no idea what he is talking about, except that she realises the danger she is in: her life stands in the firing line of his delusions and (such is the state to which he has brought her), she will readily submit (ll. 78–81). His blustering insistence now is typical of those who deep down know that they are wrong. His words suggest both that her actions are the cause of his feelings and that he cannot get her actions out of his mind. Since she is shameless, and all those like her, of her 'fact' (i.e. whores) are shameless, the more she denies it, the more she 'concerns' or calls attention to her guilt. Just as the 'brat' has been cast out, left to itself since it has no father and therefore no viable identity (although that too is her fault in his eyes), so justice for her can be no less than death (ll. 85–90).

90–107 With complete dignity, although perhaps very wearily, Hermione now explains her position. She would welcome death because all the things which gave her life meaning and value ('commodity', l. 92) have been taken away from her. Normally, a woman would have stayed in bed for a month after giving birth, partly because fresh air was regarded as dangerous to the sick. An Elizabethan audience would know that her first excursion should have been to church, both to give thanks, and to be 'purified' (for the bodily fluids involved in giving birth were regarded as 'unclean'). Instead of the privacy and seclusion that she should have enjoyed, she has been put on show in a public place. The 'open air' (l. 104) may also be another meta-theatrical reference to the play in performance at The Globe, or it may indicate (as Charles Kean interpreted it) that the trial is to be thought of as taking place in a roofless building like a theatre (see p. 136). There is deep irony in her demand to be told 'what blessings I have here alive / That I should fear to die' (ll. 106–7).

107–122 Just as she led the way to prison earlier, so now she tells Leontes to 'proceed'. But she forestalls that, coming back with vigour, with an imperious demand to be heard, and not to be mistaken: she may not care for life, but she does care deeply about her honour. If she is to be condemned on mere jealous surmise she is compelled to state that the proceedings are tyranny, 'rigour', not justice. Without actually saying so, she makes it clear that Leontes is not fit to be her judge, and it is to the rest of the court (not to him) that she turns in order to submit herself to the oracle. She will accept judgement only from Apollo.

Leontes has conducted what at times has sounded more like a marital row than a legal proceeding and it is a lord who tries to save the justice of the occasion by calling for the oracle. Hermione, as a simple matter of fact, recalls not just her parentage but her relationship to her own father, the Emperor of Russia. She wishes that he were alive and present to offer the kind of sympathetic support that a parent should offer a child, although she does not want him to exact revenge on Leontes. Her misery is absolute; she is as low and as flat in spirit as it is possible to be.

123–146   Cleomenes and Dion enter bearing the sealed oracle. Either the sword is brought to them, or more likely they are led to where it is lying. They might touch it as they swear. The oracle might be secured in a box, tied in a scroll or, in a modern dress production, simply enclosed in an envelope. As Cleomenes and Dion had hoped, this is a surprisingly non-cryptic oracular saying, except for the very last part. Now, perhaps for the first time (see note on III.ii.9.1–11 above), there is noise from the people in the court as they greet the judgement of the oracle with relief (l. 136). Leontes, however, is angry and incredulous. He will need to raise his voice to be heard above the onstage joy and hubbub. His short line, the question 'Hast thou read truth?' (l. 137) is probably designed to elicit a stunned silence. The officer perhaps falteringly holds up the oracle for him to see. But the actor playing Leontes might feel that he does not need to look at it before dismissing it and ordering the trial to continue. Having heard the oracle, the officers of the court will be unlikely to jump to his bidding, however, thus eliciting the angry self-justification 'This is mere falsehood' (l. 140). But they are in any case interrupted by the breathless, desperate entrance of a servant. Knowing that he is the bearer of bad news, he is frightened that he will be 'hated' for it (l. 142). His announcement that Mamillius has died from fear of what would befall his mother has a profound effect. Leontes immediately recognises a heavenly punishment for his injustice, and at that same moment, although there is no stage direction in F to say so, Hermione falls to the ground.

147–171   It is Paulina who tells us what has happened, and gives interpretation to the actions we (and Leontes) see. She announces that the 'news is mortal' to Hermione, that she is dying, and instructs us to 'Look down' (ll. 148–9). Where has Paulina been all this time and at what point did she come on stage? She was not allowed to visit Hermione in prison and so cannot have entered with her. It is equally unlikely that she could have been part of any ceremonial entrance with Leontes. Perhaps there was an entrance of lords, ladies and other spectators before Leontes and the officers of the court came on at the beginning of the scene, or perhaps most likely, she slipped in with

Cleomenes and Dion; given her propensity for speech, she has otherwise remained remarkably quiet up to this point.

Leontes commands that Hermione be taken out and cared for. He is still wrapped up in his own state of mind, though this time with the realisation that he has been wrong. He does not think that Hermione is in any real danger. Folio marks no exits but presumably Paulina now takes charge of taking Hermione off, while he addresses Apollo in a prayer. He might well fall to his knees asking pardon. An actor will want to come down to the front of the stage so that the bustle of the ladies' exit goes on behind him. He confesses each of his crimes and recognises the humanity and absolute honesty of Camillo, commending his willingness to risk everything.

171–181   Although there is again no stage direction in F, Paulina re-enters, staggering with unbearable emotion; she feels that she cannot breathe, that her heart is about to burst, that she needs to cut the lace that ties her bodice, but she ignores the lord who questions her as she passes. The stage is now hers for the next thirty lines. Her opening rhetorical question – 'What studied torments, tyrant, hast for me?', an explosion of 't' and 's' sounds, which cannot be hurried – is a personal attack intended to be heard by the whole court. She may still be walking towards Leontes across the stage as she says it. The monosyllabic words 'wheels, racks, fires' give a succession of equal stresses. With no unstressed syllables between them, but with the long consonantal sounds 'ls' and 'cks', they have to be said slowly and deliberately. The 'r' in 'fire', however, makes a diphthong of that word, effectively a stressed syllable, followed by the hint of an unstressed one. It is followed by the unstressed 'What'. Together this demands a silent beat on the question mark. Similar techniques (e.g. 'most, worst', monosyllables consisting of long 'o' followed by long consonant 'st') mean that each of her questions disrupt the verse line, demanding a caesura, a pause, at the question mark.

Her enumeration of all the different types of torture is an example of the rhetorical technique of copiousness. She is displaying now the skills of an orator, developed by classical authors for use in courts of law and government. She inserts herself into the proceedings, asking what punishment must be meted out to her for daring to speak to a tyrant thus, making a public spectacle of the threats he had previously made to her in the privacy of his own apartments. She assumes unprecedented power over him through her use of the familiar form 'thou', and dismisses tyranny and jealousy as marks of weakness, as indeed they are. She berates him as she might a naughty child, except that children would be more grown-up (ll. 179–81).

181–201 As so often in the language of this play, the punchline is being withheld. Leontes has previously layered one commonplace or piece of circumstantial evidence on top of another so as to convince himself of the faults of others. By contrast, she lists the possibilities of punishment for speaking thus before a tyrant, and goes through his faults and the disastrous events of the play, asserting that all are as nothing compared with the news that she has to tell. She includes in her recounting of events Leontes's attempt to involve Camillo in his crimes by demanding that he poison Polixenes, which only Leontes and the audience know about. Some editors, trying to preserve realism, have therefore placed the stage direction for her re-entry much earlier so that she hears Leontes's confession of that point, but since we know the truth of what she says, and since her function here is more like a Greek Chorus, both relaying news of an offstage event, and bringing the protagonist to an understanding of his fault (something that we will very much want her to do), we will not notice the dramaturgical sleight of hand.

Throughout the speech she has interspersed hints that things are about to get a lot worse for him. At the last minute, she turns to address the court, inviting them to share in the grief that is about to descend on them, before actually announcing Hermione's death, and moving swiftly and ironically to observe that the heavens have not yet 'dropped' their vengeance for it. The very long run-up to this very briefly delivered piece of new information means that they may not be sure what they have heard.

201–213 After the Lord's conventional expression of disbelief, Paulina now comes to expand on the death. If words are not enough she will swear it. If they do not believe her they can go and see for themselves. But since Leontes is a tyrant, she does not want him merely to repent his actions, but to despair. The setting of this play is not Christian but an Elizabethan audience will hear Christian meanings for those words: repentance might bring him salvation, but despair is a mortal sin.

213 to the end   Leontes seems set to obey Paulina's injunction to despair, although the Lord intervenes to try to reassert due protocol, blaming her for speaking too freely. This initiates a recapitulation of the gender struggle in II.iii. Some performers (and perhaps Leontes himself at ll. 231–3) have interpreted her apology here as genuine. But she again makes use of paralipsis (see II.iii.116), mentioning all the things she wants him to dwell on while pretending to advise him to forget them. As with her comment about Camillo (ll. 186–8), she cannot know that her husband is physically lost – indeed this is something the audience does not know, although we are about to find out – but she knows that Leontes had succeeded in making Antigonus take the dishonourable path, and at that moment he was lost to her (see 'we are gone', II.iii.130). Leontes asks her to lead him to where his wife and son are lying, and they leave the stage together, followed by everyone else.

Act III, scene iii

1–14   Antigonus enters carrying the baby, a box and a paper. He asks an unnamed character for confirmation that their ship has arrived in a wild and deserted part of Bohemia. This man is identified as a mariner in the SD and speech headings in the text, but his trade would be shown to an audience if he carried a chart and compasses, or a cross staff, a long stick with a sliding crosspiece for determining the angle of sun and stars, and therefore latitude. If he had just been checking their location, it would prompt Antigonus's opening question. Much has been made of Shakespeare's supposedly faulty geography, since the Kingdom of Bohemia, latterly the Czech Republic, is landlocked in the centre of Europe (but see pp. 90–4). The mariner's keen weather eye is coloured with superstition; he fears that the heavens are angry with them for what they are doing (ll. 2–6). He wants to set sail again, partly because he does not want to be too close to land when the storm breaks, and partly because he knows the land itself is teeming with wild beasts. He might be glad that his part in this dreadful affair is nearly ended; he might also be glad to have got rid of a female from his ship, since women were traditionally thought to bring ill luck to ships at sea (l. 14).

14–48   Antigonus tells the baby (and us) that he has had a dream about Hermione, which was so vivid that he felt he had seen a ghost although he does not believe in ghosts (as a good Elizabethan protestant should not). But the experience makes him suppose that Hermione is dead, the baby probably the daughter of Polixenes after all, and that Apollo wants him to expose her in her father's kingdom. He lays the child down with a written document ('character', l. 46) bearing her name, and a box that will later be identified as containing gold. We do not yet know what is in this box except that he refers to its contents in the plural as 'these' (l. 46), says they will pay for her upbringing, and that with luck there will still be some left over. Some editors also stipulate that he leaves a bundle with the baby, referring to the 'fardel' mentioned at IV.iv.754 and V.ii.3, but this is unnecessary since that fardel contains the jewel that the baby is currently wearing, and the rich 'bearing cloth' (l. 112) in which it is now wrapped.

48–57   There must be the sound of thunder at this point since he remarks that the storm begins. Thunder could be simulated by rolling a cannon ball down an inclined trough with ridges in the bottom. This might be done in the 'heavens' over the stage. There is then a 'savage clamour', a mixture of sounds including more thunder, the shouts and horns of a hunting party (ll. 56, 62–4), and in many modern productions, the amplified roar of a bear. He tells us that he has never seen the sky so dark in daytime, although there was no way of creating such a lighting effect on the early modern stage. He takes fright and his exit line 'I am gone' (l. 57) both anticipates his death and recalls Paulina's exit at II.iii.130. In the most famous stage direction of all time, he is chased offstage by a bear. The close proximity of the bankside theatres and the bear-baiting ring mean that there was a local supply of bearskins. Certainly there are other instances of actors dressed as bears in Elizabethan plays dating from the 1590s. Modern productions, wary of the humour this might evoke, tend to go for lighting effects, including enormous shadows. But horrid humour may well have been part of the original intention (see p. 118).

58–78   With the entrance of an old man dressed as a shepherd, perhaps with a smock and crook, the tone changes, not least because he speaks in colloquial prose. Although there are still sounds of hunting in the distance, the sense of danger from wild beasts and the storm diminishes rapidly. The place is not as deserted as Antigonus and the mariner thought. Some of the things that have traumatised the court in Sicily affect this man's life too – disruption of the social order and getting girls pregnant – but he has a rather more phlegmatic approach, even though he has lost a couple of sheep because of the youthful folly of the hunt.

He spots the baby and goes to have a closer look. He is struck by how pretty it is, and instantly assumes that it has been deliberately exposed because it is illegitimate. He takes pity on it, and calls for his son, who he thinks is some way off. His son takes him by surprise by hollering back loudly from onstage. His son, who as 'clown' is both country bumpkin and comic character, may be having a lark, perhaps creeping up behind him unnoticed. There is certainly space in this scene for some playfulness, or even improvisation.

78–109   The Old Shepherd wants to show his son the baby, but the Clown is too excited by the two sights he has just seen: the shipwreck; and the bear eating Antigonus. Just as the storm makes it impossible to distinguish between sea and sky so he merges his accounts of these two events, perhaps acting them out in his excitement. The Old Shepherd refers to Antigonus as 'old man' (l. 105), which is yet another instance of a character knowing things that he cannot know. He is sympathetic to another older person, but his son, in preferring him to have helped the ship, is pointing out that trying to help in either case would have been equally useless.

109 to the end   The Old Shepherd is not going to argue but can now return to his own story. The transition that began with his entrance, though interrupted by the Clown's tale of death and destruction, is now completed, 'Thou met'st with things dying, I with things new-born' (ll. 110–11). He shows his son the baby, pointing out its rich wrapper, although his imagination has only gone a few points up the social scale to 'squire', the lowest order of the gentleman class (l. 112). He tells his son to pick up the box and open it, perhaps because he himself has already picked up the baby or perhaps because he is too excited to look for himself. He recalls a moment when his fortune was told, perhaps at some country fair, that he would be 'rich by the fairies' (l. 114). His son opens the box and looks inside. He is amazed. They have never seen such wealth. The Old Shepherd's concern is to get it home as quickly as possible and without telling anyone, but the Clown says he will first go and check on Antigonus and bury whatever is left. The sheep are abandoned for the moment. They go their separate ways, each doing their good deed, the Old Shepherd with the baby and the box, telling his son to come later and fetch him if there's enough of Antigonus left to be identifiable. The Clown readily agrees on the basis that it means there will be someone else to do a bit of digging. The possible horrible laughter attached to the appearance of the bear has turned into humour indeed.

ACT IV

Act IV, scene i

1 to the end In terms of the number of lines, we are now slightly under halfway through the play. The first three acts have repeatedly shown us characters bridging stretching, or compressing both time and space (see pp. 5–6; 99). Such relativity in the way we experience time is perfectly recognisable to us as an expression of a state of mind, and in Shakespeare's *As You Like It*, Rosalind playfully explains how time seems to pass at different rates with different people (III.ii.292–324).

The character who now comes on stage identifies himself as Time and has all the attributes conventionally attached to that personification. He has not changed since history began (ll. 9–11); he has wings (l. 4), and an hourglass (l. 16). His speech also includes yet another instance of the inconsistent presentation of information, which is such a feature of the play. He asks us to remember that he has previously 'mentioned a son o'th'King's' (meaning Polixenes's son). In fact we learnt about this boy when Hermione and later Leontes quizzed Polixenes about him (I.ii.34–7, 164–72). Of course, Time as Chorus might be regarded as the 'narrator' of the entire play. Alternatively, there has been speculation that Shakespeare originally played this part himself and was here slipping between his own identity and that of the character. But these literal considerations do not tally either with the way different people remember past time differently, or with the way one experiences performance in real time. The only reality here is the audience's reality in the time and space of the theatre; it is *our* imaginative and emotional experience that matters, and *our* knowledge that has to be managed. Therefore, this passage is also a playful invitation to us to reflect on the role of our imaginations in colluding in the theatrical experience (ll. 19–23, 29–32). Practically, here, it does not matter who mentioned Polixenes's son, and the audience may indeed have forgotten about this boy. The authoritative commands to 'imagine' and 'remember' (ll. 19, 21) simply put us in the right frame of mind for what is to come.

Act IV, scene ii

1–25   The second half of the play begins in a way reminiscent of the first. It is again in prose, and again it involves Camillo, but this time he is speaking to Polixenes. It is the middle of a conversation and he has just been asking permission to return to Sicily. In the Folio he says that it is fifteen years (not sixteen) since he saw his country and some editors make an emendation. The difference could be the result of the compositor misreading xvi for xv; it could be Shakespeare being careless; but it might again be part of the pattern of discrepancies that we have noted in the play. People are often quite imprecise about large spans of time, and as one gets older, one becomes even vaguer about such things. But his comment that he has 'for the most part been aired abroad' (l. 5), suggests that he has spent most of his life away from Sicily and not just the last fifteen or sixteen years. We, of course, have no knowledge of him before Act I, scene i. In real life we interact every day with people about whose previous lives we have no knowledge whatsoever. Maybe this is a hint that there is a depth and a reality to him, and a suggestion that there are things about him, which in the last fifteen or sixteen years of close acquaintance, Polixenes now does know. It adds to our sense that we are eavesdropping on a real conversation. Camillo might, for instance, have had a previous career as a foreign diplomat. Maybe it is the ambassador's experience of foreign courts and high-level policy making that made him so indispensable first to Leontes and latterly to Polixenes (ll. 11–17), and which perhaps has resulted in an increase in Bohemia's already extensive alliances (see 'Heaping friendships', ll. 19–20; cf. II.iii.20–1). It is the kind of hint that will pass almost unnoticed by most audience members, but which an actor will seize on to help him create a convincing performance of an entirely invaluable, dependable, and experienced minister.

25 to the end   Talk of Leontes reminds Polixenes of the loss of Leontes's family, which in turn reminds him of his own. His own son, it seems, is sadly not matching up to the promise that had been shown by Mamillius, and he feels that he has lost him too. Camillo here shows his mettle as a diplomat: he has no knowledge of the prince's 'happier affairs', although he has noticed that the young man has recently been rather 'retired' from court and has been paying less attention to his princely duties than he was wont to do (ll. 29–33).

Like Polonius in *Hamlet* (Act II.i), Polixenes has set 'eyes' (spies) on his son, and has received intelligence that he has been visiting the house of a shepherd whose fortunes have inexplicably grown from nothing to a considerable estate. Camillo now admits that his own intelligence network has told him of such a person, and adds that the shepherd has an exceptionally attractive daughter. Polixenes has heard that too and fears it explains why his son has been absent. This, it appears, is the reason he does not want to lose Camillo at the moment. Camillo agrees to stay and the two men leave the stage in order to go and disguise themselves for a visit to the country.

Act IV, scene iii

1–30 In a complete change of mood, someone now enters singing a ballad-like song about spring and summer, birdsong, sex and robbery – the language includes various examples of thieves' cant ('doxy', 'pugging'). The audience will also pick up indications about him from his costume. He calls this his 'caparison' (l. 27, originally a richly ornamental cloth for a horse), and productions therefore often dress him in some kind of eye-catching, sweeping or multicoloured coat, equipped with plenty of pockets for hiding the tools of his house-breaking trade or the items he filches from the unwary. A modern dress production could equally make contemporary references to social disorder and a life lived on the road through clothing: e.g. tracksuits, hoods, or biker gear. Autolycus is a traveller, and may also have a bag ('budget' l. 20), which could later become his peddler's pack of trinkets and ballads (IV.iv.219–21), but may currently contain some stolen sheets, which he might show to us in explanation of his trade (l. 23).

Autolycus, literally 'the wolf itself' (l. 24), is the name given in Ovid's *Metamorphoses* (Book 11, 360–3) to the son of Mercury and Chione, and patron of thieves and vagabonds. Ovid describes him as a magpie, which is a bird noted for being a thieving 'snapper up of unconsidered trifles' (l. 26). Shakespeare's character, however, explains to us that he was given the name by his father because he was 'littered' (born) under the influence of the planet Mercury. He claims, however, to have had a former life serving Prince Florizel, which might make us think that Polixenes was right to be worried about his son (IV.ii.25–8).

31–48 The Old Shepherd's son now enters. He is puzzling over some arithmetic, trying to work out the amount due to him from the sale of his fleeces ('tod' is a bale of wool of a certain weight, usually 28 lbs, and 'wether', a castrated male sheep, usually in its first year). He may be trying to work it out using his fingers, but cannot do it without 'counters' (l. 35). Indeed it is not a particularly easy calculation, although 1500 sheep is a large flock yielding what was then a sizeable sum (£143 and just under 4 shillings – or £143.18 in modern currency). He turns his attention instead to what he has been sent to buy for the sheep-shearing feast: his 'sister' Perdita has given him a shopping list. This could be written down on a scrap of paper, or committed to memory. There is going to be plenty of fine food at this feast, including imported sugar, spices, currants, raisins and rice; she is 'laying it on' generously, and has even made little gifts of nosegays for the shearers. There will also be music. The shearers, who are probably travelling from village to village, plying their trade, are all, he says, good singers, no kill-joys among them; the single puritan sings his psalms to hornpipe tunes (the work songs of sailors). They have been singing songs in three parts – descant, mean (or tenor, the part that carried the tune), and bass – although in fact their voices are mostly 'means and basses'. We might suppose from all this that their performance has been lusty rather than accomplished (and this may also be an indication of the kind of music that will be performed on stage in the next scene). Nevertheless, in Bohemia, land and sea, religion and work merge in music.

49–93 While we have been enjoying the Clown's struggles with arithmetic, sophisticated music, dainty food, and flowery treats, Autolycus has been setting up his scam, stripping off and hiding his possessions, and putting on some old rags. He then lies on the ground and starts to groan and writhe to attract the Clown's attention. He pretends he has been beaten and robbed (ll. 61–3). He asks for the Clown's help in getting up because, he says, he has dislocated his shoulder, but in leaning on him closely and heavily, he manages to pick the contents of the Clown's purse. The Clown is a kind-hearted man (as we have seen in III.iii) and offers to give him some money, reaching for the purse, which is no longer full. Thinking quickly in order to stop the Clown discovering his loss, Autolycus invents a local kinsman who will be able to help him (ll. 77–83). This is his only lie, however. Everything else he says is a version of the truth, including the fact that the bedraggled man that he now pretends to be has had his clothes removed and his rags supplied by a wastrel who was 'once a servant of the Prince'. He is pretending some distant knowledge of this man, saying that he does not know 'for which of his virtues ... he was certainly whipped out of the court'. The Clown naively corrects him, stoutly asserting that not only was 'virtue' never whipped out of a court, but that it 'will no more but abide' (l. 92), i.e. can do nothing except remain there tenaciously. We, of course, know this not to be true, both with respect to the story of this play, and to courts in real life. There is perhaps, however, another meaning here, of which the Clown is completely unaware, but which does match what we know of courts and virtue more closely: 'virtue cannot but suffer (punishment)', cf. *Oxford English Dictionary*, 'abide', v. 16. A pause here while Autolycus ponders the possibilities and then corrects himself, 'Vices, I would say', will enable the audience to register at least one of these ironies, and will elicit a laugh.

93–to the end   Autolycus now expands on the various unsavoury professions of this noted footpad: whether travelling showman or bailiff. Laws banning the performance of miracle and morality plays by local guilds meant that these plays were now being performed by travelling puppet shows (motions). The choice of a play about the Prodigal Son here (see Luke, 15.11–32) suits this tempter of the young Prince Florizel. Autolycus's identification of his own name, however, might get a bigger reaction than he had bargained for; the Clown knows him for a cowardly rogue and a 'prig' (tinker and/or petty thief). In suggesting that he should have 'looked big and spit at him', he perhaps draws attention to his own large size relative to Autolycus, who in any case needs to extricate himself from this increasingly risky encounter. He pretends to take his leave, perhaps taking a few steps in the direction from which the Clown has come, again refusing all assistance. He waits until the Clown has gone on his way before scuttling back to his belongings, perhaps jingling the Clown's money ('your purse is not hot enough', l. 118) and quickly changing his clothes again, before leaving, singing, in the direction of the sheep-shearing.

Act IV, scene iv

0.1 The entrance direction in Folio lists all of the characters in the scene, including Autolycus. Autolycus certainly should not be on stage just yet. Editors are divided as to whether Perdita and Florizel should enter on their own, or closely followed by the others. Florizel's phrase 'this your sheepshearing' (l. 3) suggests at the very least that the shepherds are beginning to assemble and that there is a bustle of preparation; a gradual gathering of people would be realistic.

1–14 Florizel is dressed as a 'swain' (a young shepherd – particularly, in pastoral poetry, one who is in love). We will shortly discover that he has adopted the name 'Doricles' (see pp. 96–7). It is possible that he has raided a royal costume store, such as that kept by the Tudor and Stuart Office of the Revels, for some fanciful masque costumes for both himself and Perdita, whom he describes as Flora (Roman goddess of flowers). The miniature by Isaac Oliver, *Lady in Masque Costume*, which dates from about 1610, shows the kind of garment she might be wearing (see [http://cincinnatiartmuseum.org]). Botticelli's painting *Primavera* (Spring) shows Flora in a similar light gauzy gown, sprigged with flowers, with garlands of flowers round her head and neck, and an armful of red and white roses caught up in the front of her overskirt.

Perdita is embarrassed by the reversal of status in their respective costumes, and by the extravagance of Florizel's descriptions of her as Flora, and of the sheep-shearing as a meeting of the gods. For her, the only mitigating factor is that holiday and festival commonly include elements of folly, and that each course ('mess') at a feast might be accompanied by a different game or piece of playacting, including mock reversals of status. If it were not the custom, she would blush to see him so dressed, for she would think he had been 'sworn' (compelled, given the job) to show her a (moral) mirror, i.e. showing up her dressing-up for what it is. Theobald suggested the emendation of 'sworn' to 'swoon', which has been followed by most editors (i.e. she would faint if she saw herself in a mirror).

14–55 Florizel is euphorically in love, but Perdita fears that his father would be very angry if he happened to come across them. She is anxious about how Florizel will react; his highborn status means that he is not used to fear (ll. 17–18), but she warns him that he may not be able to withstand the king's anger (ll. 36–40). For her part, she would be embarrassed not only in being discovered, but in being caught in 'borrowed flaunts' (ll. 22–4), and she even fears being put to death (l. 40). Florizel seeks to jolly her up by reminding her of the stories from the *Metamorphoses* in which various gods disguised themselves in order to seduce young women. Some actors might want to make her laugh by imitating the sounds of bull and ram. He sees himself as Apollo, which although hubristic, contains a potential element of truth, since he has unwittingly found 'that which is lost' (see III. ii.135). But whereas the gods disguised themselves purely for sex, he means to treat her honourably and to keep faith with her (ll. 25–35). His repeated endearments ('dearest', 'my fair', 'gentle') demand some gentle and earnest caresses and he urges her to put on a cheerful expression to greet her guests who are now approaching.

55–85 The Old Shepherd comes bustling and complaining that Perdita is neglecting her duty, not matching up to the memory of how his wife used to behave on these occasions. In particular there are strangers to welcome, who we can see are Polixenes and Camillo in disguise: it is an opportunity for making friends, getting the family better known, or as we would say, 'networking'. His words are truer than he knows. With some shyness, Perdita approaches the strangers and welcomes them both, excusing her role in the proceedings; it is her father's wish. Normal protocol would require her to greet the higher status person first and editors often supply stage directions to that effect. But their disguises may have obliterated any signs of social difference. There could be some theatrical mileage in glances between Camillo and Polixenes were she to address Camillo first.

Once she has asked Dorcas for the flowers (l. 73), she seems to grow in confidence; perhaps she feels she can hide behind her role as Flora. She offers them rosemary and rue, respectively the evergreen herbs of memory, and of grace (including sorrow and repentance). Polixenes accepts, observing that they suit his advancing years, but perhaps Perdita feels she has offended them. She explains that since she is not prepared to grow 'nature's bastards', she does not grow those

flowers that would still be blooming in late summer, which would be
more suitable for their years. Ironically, in her antipathy towards bastards, she shows herself as a 'slip' (l. 84, scion or cutting of her father)
of her father. But her words carry a perhaps unconscious significance. The gillyflower (carnation, pink or other clove-scented flowers
like stocks) occurs frequently as a love token in courtly romances,
while sixteenth-century portraits of sitters holding a single carnation
are thought to signify betrothal or marriage. Marriage to Florizel is
something she desires, but thinks impossible.

85–103 Critics commonly express surprise that Perdita agrees with
Polixenes's statement that the art of the grafter is natural, while still
refusing to 'put the dibble in earth' (l. 100). Some put it down to
female 'waywardness' or the stubbornness of youth; some observe
that, although as yet she does not know it, she has been grafted onto
the shepherd's family. Grafting is the process whereby a bud of the
chosen plant is inserted into a cut in the stem of a commoner, more
vigorous rootstock. It is a method of propagation used for shrubs and
trees, and indeed gillyflower is also the name for an old, clove-scented
variety of apple, known by at least the mid-seventeenth century, and
still grown in Gloucestershire. Perdita, however, is talking about
herbaceous flowers that have become streaked either by hybridising
themselves, through (as we now understand) cross-pollination, or
by throwing a sport, or genetic mutation. Either way, they are self-
generated, and therefore in her terms 'bastards'. Since they will probably not come true from seed, they can only be propagated through
slips (cuttings), set directly in the earth. This is a different process,
although she is too polite to point it out.

Polixenes, however, also fails to understand that country gardens
cannot afford flowers grown purely for show. The point would not
have been missed by Shakespeare's earliest audiences, even those at
court. Many of the senior members of the Elizabethan government
had houses and gardens in Northamptonshire near the royal hunting
grounds. Here, on estates financed largely through sheep-farming,
gardens were laid out to be not just beautiful but practical and productive. Shakespeare himself had a smaller version of the productive
country house garden at home in Stratford. A much grander and
more fanciful style of gardening in which art was seen to be over-
coming nature was, however, in the process of being introduced

into Prince Henry's garden at Richmond (see pp. 111–12). Although the debate between Perdita and Polixenes is usually characterised as the opposition of art and nature, Perdita is better versed in the arts of gardening than he; her objection is economic and utilitarian, and perhaps critical of courtly wastefulness.

103–10 Perhaps wanting to make amends, or at least to divert the argument, Perdita then offers Polixenes and Camillo the flowers of middle summer, the 'hot' flowers blooming at sheep-shearing time, which as she delicately says, she thinks 'are given to men of middle age' (ll. 103–8). Some editors have directed that she give these flowers to the Clown and other middle-aged shepherds standing around, but this diffuses the moment into pretty but pointless flower distribution (since the Clown cannot really understand what sheep-shearers would want with nosegays, IV.ii.40), leaves the quarrel with Polixenes hanging in the air, and means that Camillo has to deliver his next lines rather vacuously to her back rather than 'gazing' directly into her face (ll. 109–10). The rosemary has not stirred anything in his remembrance, but he is strangely fascinated by her.

110–55 Refusing Camillo's compliment with another reference to winter, she turns to Florizel. She regrets she has no flowers of the spring to give to him or to the young shepherdesses, but the stories to which she refers recall her previous fear that their love is doomed. He picks up on this grim thread, and presumably she briefly throws her arms around him (l. 132), before giving her remaining flowers to him and the girls, commenting that her strange garments are making her behave with more abandon than usual (ll. 133–4). Again he praises her extravagantly, wishing that she might continue all her actions, whether dancing or selling her wares, forever because she performs them with such grace. Again, she fears that he praises her overmuch, except that she sees his true inner disposition as an 'unstained shepherd' peeping through. He calls for a dance and takes her hand.

156–81 While the young people arrange themselves (with a little rivalry between Mopsa and Dorcas for the favours of the Clown), Polixenes and Camillo stand on the sidelines, observing. Whereas Perdita and Florizel think of themselves as representatives of the natural world, whether waves of the sea or faithful turtle doves, Polixenes

finds that she is far too rarefied for this country place. Camillo observes
that Florizel has said something to her which has made her blush
('makes her blood look out', punning unwittingly on the idea of hidden
breeding l. 160), then, mediating between extremes as ever, calls her
'queen' of 'curds and cream' (l. 161).

As the music begins, Polixenes starts to question the Old Shepherd
about the young man dancing with Perdita. The Shepherd is perhaps
not entirely clear who this young man is – with reason: 'they call him
Doricles and [they also say he] boasts himself / To have a worthy feed-
ing'. He then adds rather more firmly that he has also heard this from
his own lips and believes him because he looks truthful (ll. 169–72).
But the old man clearly believes that the two young people are in love.
He is immensely proud of Perdita (ll. 178–9), and he is confident that,
with the treasure he has hidden away, she can bring any prospective
husband wealth beyond his dreams.

182–218   A servant now enters. His or, sometimes in productions
where there are female actors, her announcement that there is a
'peddler at the door' of the house does not preclude the idea that the
feast is taking place in a private area or garden outside, or, given the
unfixed locale of the public theatre stage, moving between inside and
outside. Meta-theatrically, it refers to the door of the stage.

We may assume that the music for the dancing we have just seen,
and which may still be drawing to a close, is of the very simplest kind,
depending on what is available both realistically in the shepherds'
world and in the theatre company. With a tabor (a simple drum)
struck with one hand, and a three-holed pipe in the other, a single
player could supply both beat and tune. Various styles of bagpipe
are found all over Europe and central Asia (ll. 184–5). They are particularly associated with pastoral areas since the bag, which creates a
constant supply of air, and thus enables the uninterrupted sounding
of the drone pipe, is made of sheep or goatskin. Although in the Middle
Ages bagpipers were employed by kings and barons, by the time the
play was written they were associated almost exclusively with peasant
entertainment. Ballads reporting news or telling fanciful stories were
written to be sung to well-known tunes, with choruses ('burdens',
l. 195), which enabled everyone to learn quickly and join in. They were
cheaply printed on single sheets of paper for popular sale. The collocation here between 'burden', the sexual double entendres (ll. 195–201),

and later the oblique and overt references to pregnancy (ll. 236–40, 260–9) echoes the images in Polixenes's courtly speech at I.ii.1–3.

218.1–230 Despite the inclusion of Autolycus in the stage direction at the head of the scene, F also supplies an entrance direction for him here: *Enter Autolycus singing*. The need for the editorial addition that he is '*wearing a false beard*' will become apparent at the end of the scene, where he removes his 'excrement' (hair, beard or perhaps wig, ll. 713–14). Since this actor will inevitably have taken a role in the first half of the play, probably as Antigonus, it is important that the audience do not mistake him as doubling up yet again, so he should be wearing his distinctive 'caparison' (IV.iii.27). The beard (or wig) is enough to signal that he is in disguise.

The song he is singing is one in a distinct genre based on the street cries of market traders. The items of largely female personal adornment or equipment, some of which an actor will probably want to hold up while singing about them, may be things that he has previously filched. Ironically, when Autolycus was first announced, the Clown asked whether he had any 'unbraided' (unfaded, unsoiled, i.e. new) wares (l. 204).

231–321 The triangular relationship between the Clown, Mopsa and Dorcas surfaces here again both in the rivalry between the two women (ll. 236–51, cf. ll. 162–5), and in the content of the three ballads (ll. 260–306). The possible implication is that he has made one or even both of them pregnant. Some productions have made this very visible. Perdita, however, has previously spoken a line, which in all editions is directed at Mopsa and Dorcas, in which she refers to their 'virgin branches' with the 'maidenheads growing' (ll. 115–16). Perdita, though innocent, is not ignorant of sex. She is a shepherdess, and must know about reproduction and breeding, as her dialogue with Polixenes and her guarded, though eager response to Florizel has made clear. Performers will therefore need to consider how to raise the possibility of Dorcas's and/or Mopsa's pregnancy in an audience's understanding without making Perdita ludicrously unobservant. Jealousy between the Clown's two women is written into the scene, and there is plenty of scope for additional silent business between them. It is an interesting gender reversal of the situation in the first half of the play, and the Clown is keen to keep both women happy. They exit to have it out between themselves, i.e. sing the 'Two maids wooing a man' ballad together, with a pun on sorting out their complex relationship. Either way, Autolycus aims to make a profit out of him – again.

322–340.1   The servant enters again, this time announcing the arrival of a troop of twelve amateur tumblers dressed as 'men of hair', satyrs, which perhaps s/he felicitously mispronounces as 'saltiers', those who jump or leap (ll. 322–5). Half man and half goat, satyrs are creatures of the woods, Dionysiac figures associated with sexuality and drunkenness (see Virgil, *Eclogue* VI). Three of these dancers claim to have jumped before the king, and indeed a playlet and dance of satyrs formed the antimasque in the *Masque of Oberon* (Christmas 1610–11, see pp. 114–15). One of Inigo Jones's drawings, which might relate to this masque, shows a circle of dancers in satyr costumes, each in a different leaping pose, and with elbows and knees pointed outwards in wild, inelegant fashion. Since social dances of this period normally required dancers to move in harmony together, a 'gallimaufry of gambols' (l. 326) such as the satyrs would present indicates a potentially subversive force. Significantly, the Old Shepherd wants to send them away, and it is the disguised Polixenes who asks for this performance. It therefore acts as an antimasque to his own imminent unmasking and disruption of the feast.

341–67   It is possible that the Old Shepherd takes the opportunity of the satyrs' dance to chat some more to the stranger about the possibility of Perdita's marriage to the young swain 'Doricles'. Or perhaps Polixenes initiates the conversation. One of them might gesture towards the two young people who have had nothing to say for more than a hundred lines, and who must therefore have been standing on one side all this time with eyes and ears only for each other. Polixenes's line 'O father, you'll know more of that hereafter' (l. 341) certainly looks like the closure to a conversation. Polixenes turns away from the Old Shepherd to make a private comment to Camillo: he thinks it is time to part his son from this peasant girl, seeming to refer to this last private conversation with the Shepherd 'He's simple, and tells much' (l. 343), before provocatively addressing Florizel out loud, challenging him for not buying the peddler's tat for his 'lass', suggesting that she will think he does not love her. In reply, Florizel twice makes reference to the stranger's age (ll. 354, 359), and although he seems to intend this with all the reverence due to an elder, the earlier slight problem with the flowers might encourage the actor playing Polixenes to express some annoyance, to the amusement of an audience. Florizel states that Perdita does not value such 'trifles' and takes the opportunity of the presence of a witness to pledge his love for her. He takes her hand, exploring it for softness and white-ness. Polixenes's observation that he 'seems to wash' it (l. 364), a mock use of a proverbial saying, has led some commentators to suggest that he covers it in kisses – a somewhat messy idea. For Florizel to be turn-ing it and stroking it between his own hands might better match the description. Polixenes is building up to his denouement, and there is no need to make this a private comment to Camillo, as some have suggested. Saying it out loud to all the bystanders so that Florizel also hears, makes it a deliberate attempt to embarrass his son, 'put [him] out' (ll. 364–5).

368–81 Polixenes, in character as the visitor, makes a homely reference to 'my neighbour', by which he probably means the Old Shepherd, a person with whom he, as king, wishes to have no future contact. Florizel, as Doricles, makes the announcement to the world that he would have to make in his person as prince. More than that, he declares that even if he were crowned emperor and possessed all possible attributes of beauty, power and knowledge (the three parts of the complete prince), he would not value them without Perdita's love; he would dedicate them all to her service, or [if she did not accept], disparage them all. There is an aural pun here on Perdita and 'perdition' (ll. 368–76), which Florizel may not intend. It is a rather extravagant offer, and the comments that follow this declaration explore the relationship between words and sense. Polixenes's com-ment is unlikely to indicate delight (l. 176). Rather he may think it goes beyond what the young man, even as prince, has power to deliver. Camillo, however, looks beyond the words to Florizel's feelings (l. 177). The Shepherd, who has heard the conditional 'were I crowned ... monarch' (l. 370) as expressing a metaphor for the strength of Doricles's love, and knowing about the treasure he can heap on his adopted daughter's successful suitor, asks her whether she can say she loves him too. Perdita says she cannot speak anything like as well, nor can she mean better, for she measures his feelings by her own. There is no punctuation in F after 'better', which (in modernised spelling) reads

> I cannot speak
> So well, (nothing so well) no, nor mean better
> By th'pattern of mine own thoughts, I cut out
> The purity of his.

It perhaps needs a dash after 'better', but Rowe introduced a colon, which is often turned to a full stop by later editors (thus rather disconnecting it from what follows). Modern editors also, in removing the parentheses, sometimes put a dash before 'no'. Folio's punctuation connects the 'no' with the first part of the speech, thus giving three negative words to the idea of speaking. It is an echo of the three negatives and a comparison that Leontes used after her mother's declaration of faith at her trial (III.ii.53–6). She, however, is falteringly expressing the country girl's extreme anxiety about her education. There is one negative attached to the further comparison between how well he means and how well she means. She is confident only in what she knows she thinks, and she judges him by that – also, ironically, like the king her father.

381–417   The Old Shepherd now joyfully suggests a handfasting, a ceremony in which the parties clasped hands in the presence of witnesses as a legally binding commitment to marriage. The old canon law on marriage required only the consent of the parties in the presence of witnesses, *per verba de praesenti*; neither parental consent nor a church ceremony was required for the contract to be binding. But in Reformation England, marriage without the bans being called and without a church ceremony was regarded as clandestine, and although not made illegal until 1753, could be punished in the church courts.

Florizel now compounds his earlier *faux pas* about the age of the stranger by referring to what he will inherit following his father's death (l. 385). The Old Shepherd takes his hand and Perdita's in order to perform the act of giving her to him in marriage, but Polixenes steps in, before any words can be said, to ask about the young man's father, making him confess that his father is still alive and in possession of all his faculties. Polixenes, perhaps reasonably, observes that in not telling him about his proposed marriage, Florizel is behaving in an 'unfilial' way (l. 406). He twice asks him to let him know, which an audience might momentarily hear as a rather moving plea; the Shepherd likewise urges this. But Florizel is stubborn, demanding that they proceed with the contract.

417–41 Polixenes whips off his disguise, and the reason for Florizel's refusal to consult him becomes painfully apparent. Although the young couple have not yet exchanged the vows that would make them man and wife, no one has the right to force a divorce, and Polixenes's threats of execution and physical mutilation (ll. 421, 425) are tyrannous. Yet he holds back from implementing them – partly perhaps because he does not have the back-up force to do so; partly because family members can and do threaten each other in ways that they might not ever intend to put into practice; and partly because of the nature of the play we are in. The various disguises and pieces of withheld information which have involved just about everyone on stage since the play has moved to Bohemia mean that we in the audience, who know all that there is to know (saving one important thing which will be left until the very last scene), are in a slightly superior position. Being party to every character's secret means that we are also every character's confidants and friends. Those split sympathies create a certain detachment. It is a nicely balanced situation and production choices can tip the mood in various directions.

The Shepherd's 'O, my heart' (l. 424) could be an expression of love and sympathy addressed to Perdita at the terrible accusation of witchcraft; it could be fear of a heart attack brought on by the shock of learning that Doricles is a prince. The second, more likely, option could be played for a laugh. If so, it would bring out the bathetic quality of Polixenes's threats. If what Florizel has previously vowed to Perdita is true, the threat to disinherit him (ll. 409–11) is meaningless. But there are contradictions in Polixenes's position; he admits that Perdita would be worthy of Florizel, were it not that he is a prince, yet he suggests that Florizel, in denying his birth, and perhaps in remaining silent all through this onslaught, has made himself unworthy of her (ll. 435–7). His line 'fresh piece / Of excellent witchcraft' (ll. 422–3) hinges between praise and scorn: 'fresh' means both innocent and provocative; 'piece' is both an exemplum, and a euphemism for woman of dubious virtue. We know, though he does not, that she is a piece or fragment of her mother and also extremely like her ('of a piece' with her).

And so the choice of words, although even we cannot know it yet, anticipates the descriptions of her mother's statue in the final scene: a (master) piece so fresh and lifelike that it looks like witchcraft. Polixenes makes his exit alone, having uttered the kind of comparison by opposites that we have noted in Leontes's speech: 'a death as cruel for thee / As thou art tender to't' (ll. 439–40).

441–62 Perdita's 'Even here undone' is followed by a colon in F which serves to connect it with what follows, rather than separate it (as the full stop does in many modern editions). The line suggests utter despair, but in the rest of the speech she takes charge, organising acceptance of the situation. If Florizel were standing some way away from her, it would emphasise her isolation. Perhaps the Old Shepherd is nearest, rooted to the spot after the unsuccessful handfasting. In this case the lines that follow about the sun shining on 'our cottage' as much as on the court, in which she endearingly tells us what she *nearly* said, and which are both biblical and proverbial, can be said to comfort him. She turns to Florizel telling him to leave, and then on 'queen it no inch farther' (l. 449) might remove her coronet of flowers or some other of her trappings as queen of the feast. She might even begin to walk out slowly to tend to those ewes. Camillo approaches the Old Shepherd urging him to say something lest he burst with pent-up emotion (l. 451). But the Old Shepherd feels that the incident spells his death and disgrace. Polite to his 'betters', he reproaches Florizel, putting the blame on Perdita because she has knowingly tried to marry above herself. He wishes to die and leaves the stage. The scene has reached a depth of sorrow and recrimination, which was unanticipated even fifty lines earlier.

462–73 This leaves Perdita staring at Florizel (l. 462). We might wonder why he has not yet said anything, and may even begin to think she was mistaken in him. We might ascribe those thoughts to her. But, of course, she has told him to go away. There is scope here for a pause as he registers her look, and each wonders what the other thinks. His subsequent question might come out sounding defensive, even accusatory. His 'I am but sorry' (l. 463) could sound like the start of an excuse for why he cannot stay with her. It takes a few short, slightly ambiguous phrases before his resentment at being treated by his father like a dog on a leash starts to be expressed clearly. Camillo, still wearing his disguise, steps in to urge caution. Florizel says he has no intention of going back to court, and then suddenly realises he is speaking to Camillo, who probably then takes off some part of his disguise.

474–92   Perdita again sorrowfully reproaches him; she always said this would happen. But Florizel's anger and passion have now reached frightening proportions. If he does not keep faith with her and maintain her 'dignity' as his wife, he says, then Nature might as well crush not just the whole world, but all hopes of future regeneration. Now, in fewer than twenty lines the scene has swung into wild frenzy, which Camillo's sober 'Be advised' and 'This is desperate, sir' cannot calm. He is in the grip of a 'fancy' or affection so strong that it looks like 'madness'; there is nothing under the sun or in the seas for which he would break his faith to Perdita.

492–513   Florizel expects Camillo to return to Polixenes and asks him to try to assuage his passion. He has made a hasty decision to sail away with Perdita (this is the first time we have heard that he has come by ship), and has no intention of telling Camillo where they will be going – partly because he does not know. Camillo says he wishes Florizel's spirit were more tractable to advice. But the second part of that wish 'Or stronger for your need' (l. 506) could be interpreted both as 'knew better what's best for you' and 'Even more resilient in the face of the trials to come'. While Florizel takes Perdita to one side, presumably to plan their flight, Camillo, ever the pragmatist, thinks how he can turn the situation to his own best advantage, returning to Sicily to see Leontes, as he had previously told Polixenes he wanted to do (IV.ii.4–9), while saving Florizel from danger.

513–54   Having hit on his plan, Camillo needs to take the initiative. It is therefore probably he who should approach Florizel at this point (not the other way around) thus interrupting the private conversation between the two young people and prompting Florizel's apology that his cares and need to make careful preparation ('curious business') have made him neglect his manners. Camillo then gives a perfect demonstration of the skills of the practised courtly adviser and politician. First he reinforces several times his love for Florizel's father, and then, by extension, for Florizel himself. Then he gently wonders whether the young man's 'ponderous' (well-thought through, important) and 'settled' (determined) plan might 'suffer' (allow) some slight modification (ll. 515–25). Florizel has no plan except immediate, hasty flight – which Camillo undoubtedly knows (ll. 500–2, 537–41). Camillo promises both to direct the young couple to a place where they can marry, and in their absence, bring Polixenes round, thus whetting Florizel's appetite to know more. Carefully putting all the onus on Florizel ('if you will not change your purpose / But undergo this flight', ll. 542–3), he tells him to go to Sicily and present himself and his 'fair princess' to Leontes. He is not under the impression that she is of royal birth, of course; she will be a princess because Florizel is determined to marry her (ll. 543–5). He promises to make sure that she is fittingly dressed. He then proceeds to paint a picture of how they will be received, with Leontes in the role of father asking Florizel for forgiveness. This, however, has as much to do with Camillo's current understanding of Leontes's contrite attitude to his own past actions (IV.ii.6–8) as it does with any certainty about how Leontes will behave towards the young couple.

554–84 Florizel accepts the plan wholeheartedly, asking what 'colour' (reason) he should give Leontes for the visit (l. 555). Camillo promises to write down a detailed briefing for all eventualities. In something over fifty lines, Camillo has swung the mood of desperation into one of joyful anticipation and excitement. Florizel is confident of success ('there is some sap in this', l. 565). Camillo judiciously says merely that it is better than trusting to chance, and the vagaries and dangers of sea and weather, since hardship takes the bloom off the 'complexion' and alters love (ll. 565–75). Perdita will not have her love impugned so, however: yes, hardship can take colour from the cheek but it need not alter the mind. Camillo's reply is both a compliment to her, which is the way Florizel takes it, and also a reminder of the situation she leaves behind; the Clown's children, whether by Mopsa or Dorcas will not replace her in the Old Shepherd's affection (ll. 578–9). The observation silences her and her next line will start with an apology (l. 583). In the meantime, Florizel, in blithely and rather crassly claiming that she is as much in advance of the cottage ('forward of her breeding') as she is in the 'rear' of the court (ll. 580–1), unintentionally suggests that she too is ready to breed.

Camillo diplomatically responds by complimenting her in the area in which she has previously expressed some anxiety: her education. He is conducting a dialogue in parallel, managing both of them, partly for his own ends.

585–619 Florizel, who has now relinquished all responsibility for the plan to Camillo, remembers the way in which Camillo previously saved his father, but points out that they have no suitable clothes. His use of the proverbial phrase 'to stand upon thorns' which normally means 'hopping with impatience', here also uses the word 'thorn' in the sense of impediment or difficulty (ll. 585–90). Camillo lets drop a hint of his own desires – 'my fortunes / Do all lie there' (ll. 591–2) – while reassuring him that everything is under control, as if he were the writer, producer, and director of a play. He takes them to one side, to give them further details.

This leaves the stage clear for the entrance of Autolycus. He delightedly tells us that he has sold every fake and gaudy trinket in his pack, and an actor might want to display his completely empty bag. The speech allows him to address us direct, if the actor so wishes, and to use the skills of the storyteller to act out what has happened offstage.

620–30 Camillo and the two young lovers now come forward again. One of them has just raised another practical question and Camillo reassures them that if they keep to the plan they have just devised ('by this means', l. 620), by the time they get to Sicily he will have sent letters, presumably warning of their imminent arrival and asking Leontes to write back. He will be able to show these replies to Polixenes, which will placate him. Of course we have not heard the details of how this will work. He then sees Autolycus, and with an eye to the main chance worthy of the most practised schemer, decides to make use of him. Autolycus is terrified that they have overheard the confession of his crimes and begins to tremble with fear of execution (ll. 627–9). Our delight in the scene stems from knowing that the three sets of characters on stage – Autolycus, Camillo, and the two lovers – each has a different understanding of what is going on. The story is fast spiralling into farce. With this business of the letters, however, we become aware for the first time that we ourselves may not be in full possession of the facts.

631–48   Camillo tells Autolycus that he needs him to exchange clothes
with 'this gentleman'. Even though the gentleman's clothes are more
expensive, he also offers money. Also with an eye to the main chance,
Autolycus tries to hold out for a bit more ('I am a poor fellow, sir')
before telling us in an aside that he recognises Camillo (l. 640). The
actor's tone of voice here could allow us to imagine a whole back-
story concerning Autolycus's previous encounters with Camillo at
court, although he is confident that Camillo does not recognise him.
Camillo is not prepared to pay more. Behind him, Florizel has already
stripped off his outer garments ('half flayed', l. 641). Their urgency and
willingness to overpay makes Autolycus smell a rat and he tries again
for more money. He describes the payment he has just received as
'in earnest' (an instalment or promise of a greater payment, which
also puns on Camillo's earnest manner) and pretends that he cannot
'in conscience' take it. His prevarication, and Florizel's mounting
impatience, might encourage Florizel and Camillo forcibly to take
his clothes off him on 'Unbuckle' (l. 648). Autolycus may need to do
some nifty sleight of hand to preserve his takings. Florizel now puts
on Autolycus's 'caparison' (IV.iii.27), and Autolycus dresses himself
in what Florizel was wearing for the feast (see above IV.iv.1–54). They
also exchange boots or shoes.

649–59   Now Camillo turns his attention to Perdita. He might pick
up Florizel's hat and give it to her, and take off the cloak he wore for
his own disguise so that she can 'muffle' herself and get on board the
ship unrecognised ('undescried', l. 656). She seems reluctant to get
dressed up to play yet another part. Florizel, by contrast, seems in his
element, perhaps posing in his new disguise. Since the outfit he now
wears is likely to be extreme and outlandish, we might think that the
reason Polixenes 'would not call [him] son' (l. 659), is not because he
would not recognise him, but because he looks so absurd. Camillo
decides that the hat is particularly unsuitable and probably removes
it (l. 659). The dialogue allows all sorts of comic play with hats here,
which is disguised by the stage direction supplied by Capell and common to all editions, even though it does not occur in F. This says that
Camillo *'gives the hat to Perdita'*, which rather makes nonsense of his
earlier instruction that she should take her 'sweetheart's hat' (l. 651).
He might now instead decide that that too is wrong and swap it with
his own, throwing one or both of the surplus hats back to Autolycus.

660–70 Camillo starts to shepherd Perdita in the direction of the seaside, but Florizel calls her to one side with 'What have we twain forgot?' This is another example of the scene apparently withholding information from the audience (we never discover what they talk about, and whatever it was does not feature later in the play). It also gives Camillo the opportunity to tell us what he will do after he has seen them safely on board the ship. He intends to go and tell Polixenes where they are going, in the hope that he can persuade him to pursue them. Direct address to the audience here would allow him to milk this betrayal for all its worth, before explaining that it will enable him to 're-view' Sicily (ll. 667–8). Something about the sound of these two lines, perhaps the slight salaciousness in the choice of 're-view' (with the sense of it being laid out for his gaze), and the repeated 'w' sounds which connect with 'woman's longing' (an all-consuming, pregnant craving), makes this slightly disturbing. Whether what he is proposing is best for the young people he has been counselling is less important to him than his own desire. Florizel's 'Fortune speed us' marks the end of his private conversation with Perdita, and all three exit in the direction of the ship. We know that Camillo's wish 'The swifter speed the better' means that he is thinking of his own fortune as much as theirs.

671–86 Autolycus tells us that he understands exactly what is going on. He probably taps the side of his nose to show us how astute he is (l. 673). He is evidently quite pleased with the bargain he has made. Even without the 'boot' (money), he has done well, for Florizel's clothes are better quality than his old ones. There may be some comic play, however, with the 'boot' (footwear). Perhaps he now has lightweight dancing pumps, not only unsuited to his travelling life, but capable of raising a laugh if displayed on the word 'boot'. Perhaps they are too small, causing him to hobble. One way or another, uncomfortable footwear is on his mind, and he calls Perdita a clog (encumbrance; punning on wooden overshoe).

Everyone is up to no good, it seems: the gods 'connive' (turn a blind eye to misdemeanours, or even look on with sympathy). He would not betray the prince if he thought it was honest to do so. Thus he remains true to his dishonest profession. He sees people coming and goes to hide himself, perhaps, at The Globe, behind one of the pillars holding up the stage roof.

687–708   The Old Shepherd and the Clown are carrying the box of gold, which they found with the baby, and a bundle containing the garments she was wearing. The Clown is trying to persuade his father to take them to show the king because that way they can convince him that she is a 'changeling' (l. 688, a child left by the fairies). The Old Shepherd seems reluctant to follow his son's advice. He might drag reluctantly behind his son, or hold the treasure protectively; he has kept it hidden for a long time and does not want to lose it. Either way, he seems to have recovered from his wish to die, and the Clown argues that if they prove Perdita is not their 'flesh and blood' (family), the Old Man's 'flesh and blood' (body) cannot be punished (ll. 693–5). The Clown's relentless logic has seemed surprisingly intelligent to some commentators, but he has completely mistaken the king's whim for the law of the land. In law, family members should never be held responsible for each other's crimes; to do so is tyrannous, and a tyrant is unlikely to listen to such unimportant people as he and his father. The old man is won over, however, and agrees that they should go to the king.

709–28   Wearing the prince's clothes, Autolycus perhaps thinks he is in his livery and employment. He wonders whether the 'secret things' in the 'fardel' (ll. 665, 675) might be an 'impediment' (hindrance to the prince's flight; legal term for any reason that might prevent a marriage taking place). He removes his false beard (or wig) and steps forward, adopting a mock imperious air – which in the right hands can make the word 'rustics' screamingly funny. He proceeds first to interrogate them like a comic policeman (ll. 717–20). Perhaps getting carried away, he uses the phrase 'give the lie' in two different meanings in the same sentence (overcharge for goods; accuse someone of lying, thereby inciting a challenge to a duel). In wanting to stress that he pays honestly for goods and triumphantly stressing the word 'not' the second time (tradesmen dare not accuse soldiers of lying), he inadvertently contradicts himself, which the Clown is quick enough to pick up.

729–44   Autolycus's next speech is a gift to an actor as he shows off his clothes, perhaps hobbling in his too tight shoes on 'measure of the court' (nature of the court; measured, grave steps; punning on dance step, l. 732). The Old Shepherd cannot place his manners and behaviour (l. 729) and remains sceptical, but his son is soon taken in by the airs and graces Autolycus adopts. The more fantastical and out of his daily experience they are, the more he is convinced. But Autolycus's attempt to get them to make him his 'advocate' to the king does not succeed at first.

745–805   The scene humorously pits Autolycus's posturing, in which (apparently engaged in picking his teeth, l. 752) he feigns not to hear their confused and desperate whispered asides to each other. This double comic focus is pointed up in his direct address to the audience in which he invites us to feel blessed that we are not simple like the shepherds (ll. 745–7). His misinformation that the King is not at the palace but has gone aboard a ship may be a blow to them, but he terrifies them by describing the tortures due to the Old Man and his son – once they are found. He might leer at them while dismissing those 'traitorly rascals whose miseries are to be smiled at' (l. 792–3), and might let this sink in before again offering his assistance – probably making some sign for a back-hander on 'gently considered' (l. 796). Terrified of being stung to death by wasps (l. 785), the clown is only too ready make his father offer a bribe.

806 to the end   Having extracted promises of more money from each of the shepherds, Autolycus sends them off in the direction of the seaside while he urinates ('looks upon the hedge' l. 826), and tells us that he is going to present them instead to the prince, his master. There may be something in it. If not, he has lost nothing.

ACT V

Act V, scene i

1–46   The entrance of Leontes, Cleomenes, Dion and Paulina, tells us that we are back in Leontes's court in Sicily. As described in Time's speech (IV.i.17–19), Leontes has shut himself up, grieving for his faults. Paulina is no longer the despised outsider, but the principal courtier, and the one calling the shots. The other courtiers are not the lickspittles of the past, but the responsible Cleomenes and Dion, the pair who had fetched the oracle, and who were sympathetic to Hermione. There is, however, a struggle going on between them and Paulina.

They want Leontes to remarry for the good of the state. She is determined that he should not (ll. 24–9). They express themselves in careful measured sentences, which balance remembrance of Hermione's
worth with present need. She is as passionate as before. This tension
and opposition between them might be expressed visually in the
staging, with Cleomenes and Dion on one side of Leontes and Paulina
on the other. Although there are two of them to one of her, she might
move more, and employ a greater range of vocal colour to match the
hyperbole of her speech.

As so often near the end of a Shakespeare play, dialogue takes
the form of a debate about salvation, the possibility of atonement
for sins committed, and the certainty or otherwise of forgiveness.
Cleomenes's opening speech gives one theological position: Leontes
has 'performed' like a saint, done more than enough for heaven to forgive
him; he has been penitent; he has paid for his 'trespass' (ll. 1–6). The
emphasis is on doing, which is closer to the Roman Catholic doctrine
of repentance through works than the English Church's doctrine of
salvation by faith. Leontes, however, cannot forget his responsibility
for what happened, and he cannot forgive himself for the wrong he
did to *himself* in destroying his 'sweet'st companion' and in making
his kingdom 'heirless'. He is both perpetrator and victim. Like many
victims, he cannot forgive the perpetrator of the crime. But in denying the possibility of forgiveness he is potentially committing the sin
of despair.

Paulina stresses that Hermione was unique (ll. 13–16). She points
out that the advice of Cleomenes and Dion is expressly against the
theology in place in Sicily: it denies the oracle (ll. 38–40), and opposes
the will of the gods (ll. 44–6). At the same time, she scoffs at the possibility that that which is lost will be found, for that would be 'as
monstrous to our human reason' as it would be if Antigonus were
to 'break his grave / And come again to me' (ll. 41–3). They do not,
of course, know what happened to Antigonus because the ship was
wrecked with no survivors. Nor do they know where it had sailed,
because the decision to make for Bohemia came to Antigonus in a
dream when he was already at sea. His comments on that dream
similarly expressed conflicting ideas about theology – in that case,
concerning belief in ghosts (III.iii.15–35). Paulina, however, goes further. To Christian ears, what she has just said verges on the blasphe-
mous. Christian salvation does go beyond 'human reason' and does

entail that the dead will 'break their graves', although not to return to their former lives. Raising the dead is something that only Christ can do. Prospero's claim in *The Tempest* that at his command, graves have 'waked their sleepers, oped, and let 'em forth' (V.i.49) is a mark of black magic. Paulina, however, will employ the language of forbidden magic repeatedly until the end of the play.

46–84 Paulina is confident that the kingdom will 'find an heir' which would have reminded the play's first audience that although Queen Elizabeth had died without issue, the accession of the Scottish king, James VI, to the English throne as James I had been smooth. Leontes wishes that he had always 'squared' (aligned) himself to Paulina's advice. He says he will not marry again; if he were to remarry and treat his new (but worse) wife better than he treated Hermione, she would return as an unquiet ghost to reproach him. This recurring theme marks very dangerous theological territory, which also coincides with an intractable textual crux in Folio, which reads (in modernised spelling):

> Make her sainted spirit
> Again possess her corpse, and on this stage
> (Where we offenders now appear) soul-vexed
> And begin, why to me?

There is clearly something wrong here, but the usual solutions, which tamper with the words in the parentheses, may not be the answer, particularly as they soften the potential horror. The terrifying proposition is that her 'sainted spirit' reanimates her dead body, and returns to the stage of life, where all actors are sinners, and, afflicted to the very soul, starts to question him. The line is currently a full ten syllables, but it ends with what should probably be an unstressed syllable ('vexed'), the important word being 'soul'. Other lines in this area of the play that end so usually have eleven syllables. There may, therefore, be a missing monosyllabic verb before 'soul-vexed': perhaps 'rise' or even 'shriek' (see Antigonus's dream at III.iii.35). The exchanges between Leontes and Paulina over the next fifteen lines certainly reach a frightening pitch; we cannot imagine Hermione speaking or acting in the ways described, and Leontes's wild wish to turn all the shining eyes and stars in the universe to dead coals is horrifying.

Cleomenes finds all this quite shocking: 'I have done' (l. 75). He might throw up his hands and begin to walk off, prompting Paulina to change tack. 'If my lord will marry' could be spoken to call him back, with a softer, gentler tone to Leontes, 'if you will, sir' (l. 76). Leontes agrees to let her find him a wife, but she immediately slaps him down: that will only be when Hermione lives again.

85–115   This emotional excess is only interrupted by the entrance of a servant, who says that someone calling himself Prince Florizel, son of Polixenes, accompanied by his fair princess, desires an audience with him. Leontes is surprised. This visit is completely unexpected and must be the result of some misfortune. An official visit would be planned in advance, with much display of magnificence on either side. Camillo has evidently broken his promise to send letters in advance of their arrival (IV.iv.620). Leontes asks about the size of their entourage, and about the princess. The servant replies that the followers are few and badly dressed ('mean'), but that the princess is the most 'peerless piece of earth' on whom the sun has ever shone (95). His phrase echoes Perdita's at IV.iv.444–5 and encapsulates many of the issues of the play: she is without peer (unconsciously punning on 'not noble'); she is a 'piece' (the word has previously been used in the sense of both loose woman and masterpiece or exemplum); and as a piece of earth she is both mortal and the representative of earthly beauty and the earth goddess, Flora/Demeter. But this incenses Paulina, for whom 'earth' prompts a mention of Hermione's grave. She reminds the servant that he has previously written courtly poems praising Hermione's peerless beauty. He says he has nearly forgotten Hermione, which probably gets a bad reaction from Paulina, which in turn elicits a hasty apology from him (l. 104), but not a retraction. Now turning the previous religious talk on its head, he says that this young woman is beautiful enough to start a sect, which would convert all other faiths. The word 'sect' is usually used of subdivisions of Protestantism, but the concept is preposterous, a fact underlined by Paulina's disbelieving exclamation, 'How? Not women!' (l. 109) – as if it were believable that all *men* would convert on that basis. In twenty lines we have moved from a realm of horror to one of unbelievable wonders, although as yet we can put this down to mere hyperbole.

115–51   Paulina tries to revert to the previous tone by remarking that Mamillius, had he lived, would have been a match for Polixenes's son. Just as at l. 19, Leontes asks her to stop reminding him of his lost family, but further discussion is prevented by the entrance of Florizel and Perdita. There is wonder indeed. Leontes is overwhelmed both by how much Florizel looks like his father, using the word 'print' (l. 124) as Paulina had done when describing the baby at II.iii.99–100. Florizel and his princess remind him of what his son and daughter might have looked like had they lived (ll. 131–3), although these lines have occasionally been interpreted as his memory of Polixenes and Hermione.

Florizel now gives him greetings from his father, pretending that the reason that Polixenes is not there in person is some infirmity of age (ll. 140–1). We know, of course, that this is a double falsehood; Polixenes is perfectly well, and has not sent the greetings. Leontes however is struck by what he feels as the reality of his old friend's kindness and remembers the very real wrong he did him. The sixteen year winter in Bohemia has begun to thaw as he wishes the young man 'Welcome hither, / As is the spring to th'earth' (ll. 150–1).

151–177 Leontes's attention now turns more fully to Perdita: he is, ironically enough, amazed that this 'paragon' should have been exposed to the dangers of the sea (ll. 151–5). Florizel reassures him that they are on their way back to Bohemia from her country, Libya. This remote North African country might have been chosen to explain the somewhat strange and exotic quality of her garments, allowing her to be still wearing a version of her dress as queen of the sheep-shearing. He might be a little alarmed that Leontes seems to know so much about Libya and its king, but he continues with the falsehood, adding little touches like King Smalus's tears at parting with his daughter, the fortunate southerly winds, and explaining that he has sent most of his followers on ahead to tell his father about his success. Perdita is silent throughout these falsehoods, and probably uncomfortable with them (see p. 103). Leontes feels that the gods will bless this couple's presence in his kingdom by purging it of 'infection' (see note to I.ii.281–345 above), and he might perform a fatherly blessing over them himself.

177–214 This moment of tenderness is interrupted by the entrance of a Lord. The Lord is aware that his tale would not be believed except that the proof is present in the room. He announces greetings from Polixenes, which will excite a different reaction from each of the different sets of characters on the stage. Leontes might be pleased but perhaps puzzled to have another greeting from his old friend so soon; Florizel and Perdita will look uneasy. When the Lord says that he has been sent by Polixenes to arrest his son for running away with a shepherd's daughter, there may be audible consternation, but still puzzlement from Leontes; he might wonder how this could possibly be true, and he asks eagerly where Polixenes is (l. 184). The news that Polixenes is in the city, and that he has met up with the young woman's father and brother will elicit further amazement. When Florizel blurts out that he has been betrayed by Camillo, the Lord unsympathetically adds that he can make the accusation himself to his face since Camillo too is with Polixenes. Leontes has been dearly wanting to see his former counsellor (see IV.ii.7) and seems to be more immediately excited by that than worried by Florizel's behaviour (l. 195). The Lord says that Camillo is interrogating the shepherds, 'wretches' who are trembling with fear because Polixenes is threatening them with all sorts of unspeakable deaths. This now gives Perdita cause to cry out in alarm (ll. 197–201). In an exclamation (probably to Florizel) that the gods are spying on them and will not let them celebrate their 'contract', she lets slip that they are not yet married. Leontes begins to consider this situation. He asks for confirmation that they are married. Florizel now boldly speaks the factual truth for the first time in the scene. But when asked if she is a princess, his reply, though also exactly true, is a little more roundabout, if equally defiant. Leontes wryly observes that Polixenes's speed in pursuit is likely to make the marriage 'come on very slowly'. He expresses sorrow that Florizel has broken from his filial duty and that his choice of bride, though beautiful, is not well born. It does not look as if he is about to stand up for them.

214 to the end   Perdita is overcome yet again with misery, and looking at the floor. Florizel, however, is becoming practised at this. He is much quicker than last time to declare his undying love for her, and tells her to 'look up' (cf. IV.iv.417–66). He then appeals to Leontes to remember his own feelings at the same age. The phrase 'owed no more to time than I do' has a slight echo of Polixenes's 'there was no more behind but such a day tomorrow as today' (I.ii.63–6). He asks outright for help. Leontes is indeed beginning to remember youthful sexual feelings, joking that maybe he can have Perdita if she is merely a 'trifle' (ll. 222–3), although his incestuousness is less developed than in the source. He decides to help them since they have been chaste, leading the way offstage to visit Polixenes.

It has been an emotional roller coaster of a scene and the successive revelations of the last fifty lines – though greeted variously with amazement, anger, distress and horror by those on stage – will probably have engendered a complex feeling of mingled surprise, alarm and laughter in the audience.

Act V, scene ii

1–19 A change of scene marks another complete change of tone and style. Verse gives way to prose, and an onstage representation of extreme emotions to a slightly detached, even amused retelling of an event that has taken place offstage. The scene we are watching can be considered as taking place somewhere in the city, near the chamber where the scene we are hearing about has been taking place.

Perdita's birth father, adopted father (and brother), and prospective father-in-law, have at last learnt what we, the audience, have known all along. Rather than having to witness those characters' emotions, however, we are free to imagine them. The gentlemen have no personal emotional investment in the story. Their near disbelief in the fantastic tale they are telling means that we can watch with some amusement as they gradually piece it together. The main play thus briefly becomes a play-within-the play, played out in our imaginations. This scene explores ideas about sound and gesture, and the aural and the visual, which both inform and derive from Shakespeare's experience as a dramatist.

Each gentleman has a different level of knowledge of what has taken place. Autolycus, however, has a personal financial interest in the outcome. By appearing insouciant and courtly, he hopes to glean information that he might be able to use to his own advantage. The First Gentleman says he was ordered out of the chamber early on in the meeting between the kings and the shepherds and is only able to tell us what he thinks he heard (that the Old Shepherd found the child). He has certainly seen Leontes and Camillo overwhelmed to meet each other again. He is unable to tell just by looking at them whether their emotion derives from sorrow or from joy, yet their gestures and silence seemed to tell an eloquent tale (ll. 13–14).

20–29 The Second Gentleman comes in with the news that Leontes's daughter is found: even ballad-makers, he says, will not be able to match the wonder of this story (see I.ii.1–27 above). Ironically, we are given a name for this particular gentleman: Rogero – also the title of one of the most popular and ubiquitous of ballad tunes in early modern England. But as his reference to the fanciful inventions of ballad makers makes clear, he does not entirely believe what he has heard, 'the verity of it is in strong suspicion' (ll. 28–9). He is also not a reliable witness, for he does not even need to have been in the chamber to have heard talk of 'Nothing but bonfires' (l. 22); he could be just reporting a rumour.

30–78 The Third Gentlemen, Paulina's steward, is a little closer to the main characters in the story. He sets out Shakespeare's technique for this scene, for we too have 'lost a sight which was to be seen, cannot be spoken of' (ll. 42–3). Ironically, we can only see it by hearing him speak of it. The paradox in telling the thing that cannot be told is that we (and the onstage audience) see the things we have been prevented from seeing. The Third Gentleman's own disparagement of the ability to tell adds to the sense of wonder. Like popular romance literature, it piles one episode on another; no one believes it and they may even stop listening (ll. 61–3). The news that Antigonus was 'torn to pieces with a bear' (l. 63) may well, therefore, be greeted by the gentlemen with hoots of derision, both at the event itself and at the 'innocence' of the Clown who has retold this story. This slowly cools to sympathy with knowledge of the destruction of the ship and its sailors, and lastly to admiration for the way in which Paulina handles her mingled grief (for the loss of her husband) and joy (at the finding of Perdita; ll. 69–78).

79–91 This paradox culminates in an observation by the First Gentleman (who had been excluded from witnessing the event) that the 'dignity of the act was worth the audience of kings and princes, for by such was it acted' (ll. 79–80). Of course, some of the actors in this story are shepherds, while in real life all the actors are common players.

Despite being deeply affected by what he saw, the Third Gentleman knows that he is not personally involved. The event 'angled' for his eyes, 'caught the water but not the fish' (ll. 82–3). He wept, but his own life is unaffected, and he can joke about his tears (as he does here) even while acknowledging them. The strange phraseology draws attention to itself. It is an echo of Leontes's jealous metaphor for being cuckolded, to have one's 'pond fished' by one's neighbour (I.ii.196), and also an exact metaphor for the strange reality of being emotionally involved while watching a mere play. If his heart 'wept blood', it is an acknowledgement of how much he felt, but of course it is also, in a sense, what hearts do all the time. Even without knowledge of the role of the heart in the circulation of the blood, any butcher or cook knows that a heart is full of blood.

92–111 The Third Gentleman at last begins to tell us something we do not know: that the court party has gone to see a statue of Hermione that Paulina has commissioned from the renowned Italian artist Giulio Romano. Modern editorial punctuation of this passage, by converting F's colons into full stops, invariably leaves the sentence beginning 'The Princess' incomplete. It is better to regard everything after 'Paulina' (l. 94) and before 'Thither' (l. 101) as in parentheses, treating the whole speech as a single sentence: 'The Princess, hearing of her mother's statue, which is in the keeping of Paulina ... thither with all greediness of affection, are they gone and there they intend to sup'. The Gentlemen do not want to be left out, for this time they will be allowed access (l. 109), and eagerly make their way off.

112–22 All the talk of wonder and noble emotion now comes down to earth with a bump as Autolycus gives a slightly disgruntled, matter-of-fact and colloquial account of his attempt to tell Florizel about the Shepherds and their 'fardel', plus a rather more realistic picture of Perdita, on a ship, throwing up. Autolycus laments that if she had not been seasick – and Florizel little better – he might have been able to get the Old Shepherd and his son to disclose the contents of their bundle before they ever got to Sicily. Philosophically, however, he reflects that this would not have matched his normal discreditable behaviour (ll. 120–2).

123–36 The Old Shepherd and his son enter. They have been granted gentlemanly status and are dressed up accordingly. Displaying his new finery, the Clown immediately begins to pick a quarrel with Autolycus

on the grounds that he had refused to fight him previously because
he was no gentleman. In giving him 'the lie' (l. 132) he may consciously
recall Autolycus's words at IV.iv.722–6. We (and Autolycus) might
remember that he had previously told a disguised Autolycus that
he should have 'looked big and spit' at the notorious thief who had
beaten him. On that occasion, Autolycus had replied (probably truth-
fully) 'I am no fighter' (IV.iii.105–6), although he is also unlikely to be
frightened here by the Clown's swagger.

137 to the end　　The Clown is enjoying his new role in the social
pecking order, calling attention to his kinship with the royal family
(ll. 138–42), relishing the freedom to swear like a 'gentleman' (ll. 157–8),
and lording it over Autolycus, who he says, has no right to get drunk
unless he can prove himself to be a 'tall' (capable) fellow (ll. 161–70).
A contemporary audience would have enjoyed the satirical reference
to the buying and granting of titles under James I (see pp. 92–3).

In his brief mutterings of agreement and acquiescence, Autolycus
seems to have been humbled. An actor will want to make a decision
whether or not this is genuine. The Clown is so wrapped up in his
new clothes and manners that there is plenty of scope for Autolycus
to indicate to the audience with a look or a gesture that he is merely
biding his time, and looking for future advantage for his capable,
pickpocketing 'hands'. This is an instance where there might indeed
be 'language in … very gesture' (ll. 13–14) on the part of all three of the
characters on the stage, because the Old Shepherd's new clothes and
status are strange and uncomfortable to him, and he is concerned
about a possible loss of the family's previously high moral values:
'How if it be false, son?' (l. 159).

At the end of the scene, the Clown is in full flow, getting himself
in a tangle over the phrase 'tall fellow' (with a likely additional visual
joke here if the actor playing Autolycus is not particularly tall, see
IV.iii.105 above). Although some commentators interpret the word
'Hark' as merely 'Listen to me', he is probably interrupted by an offstage sound effect (perhaps a trumpet flourish and/or vocal noise and
cheers), which tells him that their 'kindred are going to see the Queen's
picture', i.e. funeral effigy (ll. 171–2, see pp. 109–10). His promise to
Autolycus that they will be 'good masters', however, indicates that
he has not yet lost all sense of his previous generosity.

Act V, scene iii

0.1 The previous scene saw the three Gentlemen, the two Shepherds and Autolycus leaving the stage to go and see Hermione's statue, but they are not required to speak in the final scene. The composite stage direction in F at the head of the scene lists all the speaking parts in order of rank or seniority, adding after a colon '*Hermione (like a statue:) Lords, etc.*' The 'etc' has not featured in other stage directions in the play, and it is likely that all the available actors in the company are on stage, including all those characters from the previous scene. The statue is screened by a curtain (l. 59), as was not unusual at the time for particularly treasured items. On the Globe stage it was probably positioned behind a curtain in the central entrance or 'discovery' space.

Some productions and commentators envisage the scene played out in a chapel in Paulina's house (see l. 86), with the statue of Hermione as a funerary monument. Such statuary, even if the subject is depicted as alive, is invariably sombre with a stiff, static pose, quite unlike all the descriptions of the statue in the text. Paulina seems to be a collector of curiosities (l. 12) and works of art – as was just beginning to be fashionable among England's wealthiest aristocrats when the play was written. The gallery in her house is like an art gallery or museum, and the scene can be envisaged as taking place in a side alcove dedicated to Hermione's memory, just as chapels dedicated to particular saints are positioned as gated or screened alcoves to the sides of Christian church aisles or naves (cf. Hermione's 'sainted spirit', V.i.46–84 above).

1–20 Leontes thanks Paulina for everything she has done, but she demurs, and then gives the subject's expected thanks to the sovereign for honouring her with a visit. But, as Leontes points out, although they have taken much interest and delight in seeing her collection of 'singularities' (l. 12), which might include objects of natural history and ancient history as well as contemporary art, they are anxious to see the real reason for their visit, the statue of Perdita's mother. It might be imagined that Perdita herself has taken little interest in the other exhibits, and may even be displaying some impatience, which would prompt Leontes's reference to her desire rather than his own (l. 13). Paulina, however, has presumably been deliberately withholding the promised statue, so as to bring them to an even more eager state of anticipation. She warns them to expect something extraordinarily lifelike, before drawing the curtain to reveal it (ll. 18–20).

21–42 The appearance of Hermione's statue is greeted with utter silence on stage (l. 21), which is another reason for supposing that the '*Silence*' in the F text at her trial is a stage direction and not an order (see note on III.ii.10 SD above). The choice of Giulio Romano as the artist indicates that it should look as if on the point of speech and movement (see ll. 34–5, 23; pp. 108–11). Leontes still believes that Hermione should chide him for his 'evils', but now he recognises that she was never the sort of person who would 'chide'. The effect the statue is having thus contradicts the dialogue at V.i.56–67.

42–8 While Early Modern English protestants would have regarded it as 'superstition' (l. 44) to kneel to the effigy of a saint asking for blessing or intercession (cf. V.i.57, and V.iii.0.1 SD above), some of them certainly would have thought it desirable for a child to kneel to a parent in the way that Perdita now does. The audience is as likely to be close to tears of sympathy as the Third Gentleman in the previous scene (V.ii.83), but we are also likely to be pretty sure that the statue is being played by a living actor. Therefore, when Perdita expresses in word and gesture the need to touch it, and is hastily prevented in the nick of time by Paulina on the grounds that the painted parts are not dry, we are equally likely to smile (ll. 46–8). The words used to describe the statue throughout recall the words used to describe Hermione just after the moment of her supposed death (III.ii.203–6). Then she had no colour in her lip or lustre in her eye, no breath in her body and no warmth to the touch.

49–85 Leontes becomes more and more affected by what he sees, to the extent that first Camillo then Polixenes need to comfort him, and probably move towards him to do this. Paulina starts to draw the curtain to hide the statue on the grounds that he is so overwrought that he will start to imagine that it moves (l. 61). We have probably reached the limit of time that an actor in full view can remain completely motionless, so that when Leontes begins to detect breathing (ll. 64), our visual experience may well match his.

He then sees the veins beneath her skin, and life in her eye (l. 67). The eye is commonly thought of as a window on the mind or soul, which is in turn commonly characterised in movement, stirred by emotion. Thus, although he knows the statue's eye to be painted, set, fixed, it appears to reveal inner life, spirit, 'motion'; 'By motion, the painters meane that comelines and grace in the proportion and disposition of a picture, which is also called the spirite and life of a picture' (Haydocke, 1. 23, cited in *Oxford English Dictionary*). The artistry of the statue 'mocks' (matches; imitates) the reality of human physical existence, 'we are mocked with art' (l. 67). In most productions, the line is delivered as part of the wonder of the scene. But in Declan Donellan's production, Leontes delivered it angrily, suggesting in one critic's view that the statue was fraudulent or perhaps that the thing that he most wants, a living Hermione, is cruelly denied him in this lifeless imitation of her. This, however, does not sit happily with Paulina's suggestion that 'He'll think anon it lives', his subsequent wish for the 'pleasure of that madness', and his desire to be 'afflicted further' (l. 70–7). He is now convinced that he can smell her sweet breath and moves to kiss her. Again Paulina stops him, and asks if she should draw the curtain. Both Leontes and Perdita are adamant that they want to continue to gaze at the statue.

85–103 Having thereby convinced herself that the time is right, Paulina embarks on the last stage of her plan. If everyone is prepared for it, she can 'make the statue move indeed, descend / And take you by the hand' (ll. 87–8). This would be a witchcraft requiring the assistance of spirits, and according to King James's own book, *Daemonologie*, all spirits were, by definition, devils. She again asks for confirmation that everyone is prepared for this. Those who think it 'unlawful' (l. 96; cf. II.ii.12) should depart. In contrast to the event reported in V.ii, no one is banished from the chamber, indeed Leontes decrees that everyone should stay. Paulina calls on her probably hidden band of musicians to begin to play, so that the swelling sound should strike life into the 'statue'. But the real effect is on the audience, both on and offstage for music with spoken voiceover is emotionally very powerful. Hermione does not move instantly; Paulina has to urge her gently several times but this allows the music and the wonder of the moment to register with the audience. Perhaps, realistically, she is suffering from 'numbness' (l. 102) from having held a pose for so long, and Paulina's line could certainly be delivered with a slight smile. As so often in this play, there is more than one interpretation for what we see.

103–11 She moves. They start in surprise. Leontes is said to 'shun her' (ll. 104–5). Perhaps he shrinks back into himself, frozen with a certain horror at the 'magic' he is witnessing, for Paulina has to tell him to take Hermione's hand. She refers back to the time when Leontes wooed Hermione, when it was he who had to wait for her to respond (cf. I.ii.104–6). The essential pathos of this scene is that no one can put back the clock. Neither Mamillius nor Antigonus will be brought back to life; their time has gone. But this staging of the awakening of a statue allows another turn of Time's glass in a reprise of some of the ideas, emotions and gestures that we saw or heard about earlier in the play. Leontes takes Hermione's hand and finds that it is warm. The very real physical emotion of the scene is expressed in bodily terms as 'Lawful as eating' (l. 111, cf. V.ii.102). We commonly feel basic emotions as flutterings in the stomach, and eating is the very basis of life, although the bear's dinner was the death of Antigonus (III.iii.103, 126–7). But this natural, healthy response to the belly is in contrast to the diseased obsessions of the beginning of the play (cf. I.ii.110–48 above).

111–22 Hermione and Leontes stand motionless and speechless in each other's arms for some ten lines. Polixenes and Camillo describe the gesture. She embraces him. But more than that, she 'hangs about his neck' (l. 113). The verb 'hangs' implies duration, which in turn implies that the stage picture is still and the spoken comments interspersed with silences (apart from the music, which might continue up until the moment that Hermione begins to speak at l. 122). Camillo wants to hear her speak to prove that she is genuinely alive, perhaps because moving automata were quite familiar in aristocratic renaissance houses and gardens. But while the implied stage directions in the dialogue are clear, the meaning of the gesture we see requires interpretation. We do not know whether her embrace shows warmth and love or resignation and sorrow, or a complex mixture of all those emotions. The speaking, when it comes, is to her daughter, not to Leontes. Can she really forgive him for what he did? As so often at the end of a Shakespeare play, there is no definite answer or message. What we would want her to feel depends a great deal on who we are as individuals, and the most heart-rending productions are those which preserve that ambiguity for their audiences to puzzle over. Accordingly, Paulina refuses to give a straight answer as to how Hermione has been secretly preserved alive for so long or, indeed, whether she has not been brought back to life, 'stol'n from the dead' (l. 116). A rational real-life explanation would be as unbelievable as a magic romance story, and would be 'hooted at / Like an old tale' (ll. 17–18). But this statement that it is unbelievable, of course helps us to believe it. This is the real Hermione, still living.

Paulina at last decides that it is time to intervene and asks Perdita to kneel once more to her mother. In another echo of the language of earlier parts of the play, Paulina has perhaps the most moving line of all: 'Turn, good lady, / Our Perdita is found' (ll. 121–2; cf. 'good Queen', II.iii.58–60; I.ii.220). Another turn of Time's glass has brought mother and daughter together, so that which was lost is finally found. But it is perhaps the reference to 'Our' Perdita that is so affecting, with its implication that children are a community responsibility, not just a personal parental one. The safety of the baby was a duty, which the court as a whole, and not just Leontes, had signally failed to grasp.

122–to the end Realistically, Hermione wants to know the story of how Perdita was preserved and found. But we have both seen and heard this at least twice. Maybe Perdita takes breath to launch into it when Paulina intervenes to stop her. The characters have all the time in the world, but time is too short for us to want to hear it again. We might smile with some relief. She tells them all to go and 'partake' in their various stories of preservation offstage, while she goes to lament her husband, until she too is 'lost', dead (l. 136). Previously the word that had connected her and her husband in that way was the more final 'gone' (cf. II.iii.130; III.iii.57). But we now learn for the first time of the other side of the pact between Leontes and Paulina: if she finds him a wife (cf. V.i.76–84), he will find her a husband.

Certainly, if a 'marriage of true minds' is indeed the recipe for successful union (see Sonnet 116), there can be no more suited couple than Paulina and Camillo, who have both shown their absolute integrity and loyalty for so long, although both have also been duplicitous. The notion that she can be married off like this, however, has been anathema to some critics, and has occasionally been cut in performance. The phrase 'whose worth and honesty' refers grammatically to Camillo (l. 145). It is as if Leontes, who already 'partly' knows Camillo's mind on this matter, is persuading Paulina of his worth. But marriage is a sacrament that must be freely entered into by both parties. Camillo's gesture in offering his hand, and hers in (presumably) accepting it, is a little silent play that can be staged over the next few lines. Leontes's line 'Let's from this place' (l. 147) might even be delivered with some slight embarrassment as a means of giving them the space and privacy to do just that. But in turning away he catches sight of Hermione and Polixenes. The F line reads 'What? looke upon my Brother:' (l. 148). Is she looking at him? Or is she being careful not to do so? The former is more likely, given what we know of her character, although the change of focus is so abrupt that even spectators may not be sure what they have seen. In one sense it does not matter because this entire play has been predicated not on what she was doing but on the interpretation put on her actions by her observing husband. The question or the outcry, 'What?' (since the Folio frequently uses question marks to indicate exclamations), is enough to freeze the blood of everyone, both on and off stage, as we all recall his earlier jealousy. Now, however, he might join their hands, or clasp their already-joined hands in his. Maybe he then performs that same gesture on each of the soon-to-be-married couples on the stage, before asking Paulina to lead the way. Or maybe, he leads Hermione over to greet her future son-in-law.

How, then, do they leave the stage? Paulina and Camillo, Perdita and Florizel, as couples? Polixenes and Leontes each hand in hand with Hermione? Or do Leontes and Hermione follow Paulina, leaving Perdita's adopted father and father-in-law to cross the class divide and walk together? And who is the last person to leave the stage? Autolycus? The tone is joyous and positive but in Leontes's use of the passive tense 'we were dissevered', we can, if we want, discern the beginning of the rewriting of history: the removal of his agency and the placing of responsibility for events on the workings of time. Maybe that is a necessary part of the healing process. But as always, Shakespeare leaves us with the hint that although the play may be over, the story will continue, and that these things happen – again and again.

3   Sources and Cultural Context

The main source for Shakespeare's play is Robert Greene's prose romance, *Pandosto, the Triumph of Time*. Subtitled *The History of Dorastus and Fawnia*, it was published in 1588 and proved the most popular of all Greene's works, appearing in six editions by 1609, and reprinted frequently thereafter. Shakespeare relies heavily on Greene's story for the first half of his play, adopting wholesale Greene's account of the King's behaviour – his unfounded jealousy, fear of being poisoned, sleeplessness, and murderous intent towards both his wife and the person he regards as his rival. Greene is also the origin of some striking phrases, for example 'rigour and not law' and 'refer myself to the divine oracle' in Hermione's speeches to the court (cf, III.i.113–14). But the differences are also illuminating. Shakespeare swaps around Bohemia and Sicily (see below pp. 90–4); his king denies the truth of the oracle; his queen becomes pregnant much earlier in the story, and does not die. Rather than continuing the narrative of the baby girl's upbringing, he skips over those sixteen years, settling into a succession of different modes of story telling for the Bohemia scenes and the subsequent return to Sicily. As a result, and despite being one of the longest in all his plays, the sheep-shearing scene contains relatively few story developments – although those few are life-changing for the characters concerned. Instead, he presents a range of different types of sexual and marital states: the romantic chaste love of Perdita and Florizel/Doricles; the idea of marriage as property right, shared at opposite ends of the social scale by Polixenes and the Old Shepherd; the Shepherd's memory of his homely hospitable wife; the contested loves of Mopsa, Dorcas and the young shepherd; Autolycus's bawdy songs and ballads; and threaded throughout, repeated reference to 'breeding' as both sexual act and social status. Most of these are also found in Greene, but the effect there is rather different. Greene reports and seemingly endorses the prince's sense that his love for the shepherdess is 'fancy', 'base desires', 'crooked desires', 'wretched fortune', 'wilful folly', and against his 'honour'. His characters repeatedly reflect that their misfortunes stem from their rashness in contravening parental wishes and social distinction. Similarly, while Leontes is immediately struck by the appearance of his grown-up daughter, and even sexually excited by her, Greene's King Pandosto goes so far as to try to seduce the shepherdess, throwing the prince into prison when she refuses. It is for these reasons alone that he is called tyrannous. Leontes excuses himself by saying that he was thinking of Hermione, and that the young couple remind him of what he has lost. He decides to help them because of their virtue before any of the characters know her identity.

Greene's story is locked into the social structures of its time. The only solution to the characters' predicaments is the final revelation of the shepherdess's royal birth. Shakespeare, however, presents genuine social questions that are still relevant. He introduces the notion of tyranny early in the plot and, with the need to create a character who can arrange Hermione's concealment, he creates an immensely strong female presence in Paulina. From the perspectives of three different estates – royal, noble and peasant – Hermione, Paulina and Perdita in turn challenge traditional male power. His comic presentation of the newly gentrified shepherds, particularly the young shepherd, is more a commentary on lack of sense than lack of breeding, and a satire on those for whom social status is important. While Shakespeare's clown, comically, thinks it is a mark of breeding to swear, Greene's starts demanding bribes – a characteristic that Shakespeare gives instead to the rogue, Autolycus.

Selections from *Pandosto*

In modernised spelling and punctuation

Among all the passions wherewith human minds are perplexed, there is none that so galleth with restless despite as the infectious sore of jealousy; for all other griefs are either to be appeased with sensible persuasions, to be cured with wholesome counsel, to be relieved in want, or by tract of time to be worn out (jealousy only excepted), which is so sauced with suspicious doubts and pinching mistrust, that whoso seeks by friendly counsel to raze out this hellish passion, it forthwith suspecteth that he giveth this advice to cover his own guiltiness. Yea, whoso is pained with this restless torment doubteth all, distrusteth himself, is always frozen with fear, and fired with suspicion, having that wherein consisteth all his joy to be the breeder of his misery. Yea, it is such a heavy enemy to that holy estate of matrimony, sowing between the married couples such deadly seeds of secret hatred, as Love being once razed out by spiteful distrust, there oft ensueth bloody revenge, as this ensuing history manifestly proveth, wherein Pandosto (furiously incensed by causeless jealousy) procured the death of his most loving and loyal wife, and his own endless sorrow and misery.

In the country of Bohemia there reigned a king called Pandosto, whose fortunate success in wars against his foes, and bountiful courtesy towards his friends in peace, made him to be greatly feared and loved of all men. This Pandosto had to wife a lady called Bellaria, by birth royal, learned by education, fair by nature, by virtues famous, so that it was hard to judge whether her beauty, fortune or virtue won the greatest commendations. These two, linked together in perfect love, led their lives with such fortunate content that their subjects greatly rejoiced to see their quiet disposition. They had not been married long, but Fortune (willing to increase their happiness) lent them a son so adorned with the gifts of nature as the perfection of the child greatly augmented the love of the parents and the joys of their commons in so much that the Bohemians, to show their inward joys by outward actions, made bonfires and triumphs throughout all the kingdom, appointing jousts and tourneys for the honour of their young prince ... This solemn triumph being once ended, the assembly, taking their leave of Pandosto and Bellaria, the young son (who was called Garinter) was nursed up in the house to the great joy and content of the parents.

Fortune envious of such happy success, willing to show some sign of her inconstancy, turned her wheel and darkened their bright sun of prosperity with the misty clouds of mishap and misery. For it so happened that Egistus, King of Sicily, who in his youth had been brought up with Pandosto, desirous to show that neither tract of time nor distance of place could diminish their former friendship, provided a navy of ships and sailed into Bohemia to visit his old friend and companion, who hearing of his arrival went himself in person, and his wife Bellaria, accompanied with a great train of lords and ladies, to meet Egistus, and espying him, alighted from his horse, embraced him very lovingly, protesting that nothing in the world could have happened more acceptable to him than his coming, wishing his wife to welcome his old friend and acquaintance, who to show how she liked him whom her husband loved, entertained him with such familiar courtesy as Egistus perceived himself to be very well welcome. ...

... Pandosto entertained Egistus and his Sicilians with such banqueting and sumptuous cheer so royally as they all had cause to commend his princely liberality. ... Bellaria, who in her time was the flower of courtesy, willing to show how unfeignedly she loved her husband by his friend's entertainment, used him likewise so familiarly that her countenance betrayed how her mind was affected towards him, oftentimes coming herself into his bed chamber to see that nothing should be amiss to mislike him. This honest familiarity increased daily more and more betwixt them, for Bellaria, noting in Egistus a princely and bountiful mind adorned with sundry and excellent qualities, and Egistus, finding in her a virtuous and courteous disposition, there grew such a secret unity of their affections that the one could not well be without the company of the other, in so much that when Pandosto was busied with such urgent affairs that he could not be present with his friend Egistus, Bellaria would walk with him into the garden, where they two in private and pleasant devices would pass away the time to both their contents. This custom still continuing betwixt them, a certain melancholy passion entering the mind of Pandosto drove him into sundry and doubtful thoughts. ... He considered with himself that Egistus was a man and must needs love, that his wife was a woman and therefore subject unto love, and that where fancy forced, friendship was of no force.

These and such like doubtful thoughts a long time smothering in his stomach began at last to kindle in his mind a secret mistrust, which increased by suspicion, grew at last to be a flaming jealousy that so tormented him as he could take no rest. He then began to measure all their actions and to misconstrue of their too private familiarity, judging that it was not for honest affection but for disordinate fancy, so that he began to watch them more narrowly to see if he could get any true or certain proof to confirm his doubtful suspicion. While thus he noted their looks and gestures and suspected their thoughts and meanings, they two seely souls, who doubted nothing of this his treacherous intent, frequented daily each others company, which drove him into such a frantic passion that he began to bear a secret hate to Egistus and a louring countenance to Bellaria, who marvelling at such unaccustomed frowns, began to cast beyond the moon and to enter into a thousand sundry thoughts which way she should offend her husband, but finding in herself a clear conscience, ceased to muse until such time as she might find fit opportunity to demand the cause of his dumps. In the meantime, Pandosto's mind was so far charged with jealousy, that he did no longer doubt but was assured (as he thought) that his friend Egistus had entered a wrong point in his tables and so had played him false play; whereupon desirous to revenge so great an injury, he thought best to dissemble the grudge with a fair and friendly countenance, and so under the shape of a friend to show him the trick of a foe. Devising with himself a long time how he might best put away Egistus without suspicion of treacherous murder, he concluded at last to poison him, which opinion pleasing his humour, he became resolute in his determination and the better to bring the matter to pass he called unto him his cupbearer, with whom in secret he brake the matter ... His cupbearer, either being of a good conscience or willing for fashion sake to deny such a bloody request, began with great reasons to persuade Pandosto from his determinate mischief ... And that if he now should, without any just or manifest cause, poison him, it would not only be a great dishonour to his majesty, and a means to sow perpetual enmity between the Sicilians and the Bohemians, but also his own subjects would repine at such treacherous cruelty. These and such like persuasions of Franion (for so was his cup-bearer called) could no whit prevail to dissuade him from his devilish enterprise, but remaining resolute in his determination, ... he began with bitter taunts to take up his man and to lay before him two baits: preferment and death, saying that if he would poison Egistus, he should advance him to high dignity; if he refuse to do it of an obstinate mind, no torture should be too great to requite his disobedience. Franion, seeing that to persuade Pandosto any more was but to strive against the stream, consented as soon as opportunity would give him leave to dispatch Egistus, wherewith Pandosto remained somewhat satisfied, hoping now he should be fully revenged of such mistrusted injuries, intending also as soon as Egistus was dead to give his wife a sop of the same sauce and so be rid of those which were the cause of his restless sorrow. ... Franion being secret in his chamber, began to meditate with himself in these terms:

'Ah Franion, treason is loved of many, but the traitor hated of all; unjust offences may for a time escape without danger, but never without revenge. Thou art servant to a king and must obey at command, yet Franion, against law and conscience, it is not good to resist a tyrant with arms, nor to please an unjust king with obedience. ...'

... seeing either he must die with a clear mind or live with a spotted conscience, he was so cumbered with diverse cogitations that he could take no rest, until at last he determined to break the matter to Egistus. ... Lingering thus in doubtful fear, in an evening he went to Egistus' lodging. ... Franion made manifest the whole conspiracy which Pandosto had devised against him, desiring Egistus not to account him a traitor for betraying his master's counsel, but to think that he did it for conscience. ... Egistus had not fully heard Franion tell forth his tale, but a quaking fear possessed all his limbs, thinking that there was some treason wrought, and that Franion did but shadow his craft with these false colours; wherefore he began to wax in choler and said that he doubted not Pandosto since he was his friend, and there had never as yet been any breach of amity; ... he knew not therefore any cause that should move Pandosto to seek his death, but suspected it to be a compacted knavery of the Bohemians to bring the king and him at odds.

Franion staying him in the midst of his talk, told him that to dally with princes was with the swans to sing against their death ... therefore his majesty did ill to misconstrue of his good meaning, since his intent was to hinder treason, not to become a traitor. ...

Egistus hearing the solemn protestation of Franion, ... gave great thanks to Franion, promising if he might with life return to Syracuse, that he would create him a duke in Sicily, craving his counsel how he might escape out of the country. Franion, who having some small skill in navigation, was well acquainted with the ports and havens and knew every danger in the sea, joining in counsel with the master of Egistus's navy, rigged all their ships, and setting them afloat, let them lie at anchor, to be in the more readiness when time and wind should serve. ...

Fortune although blind, yet by chance favouring this just cause, sent them within six days a good gale of wind, which Franion seeing fit for their purpose, to put Pandosto out of suspicion, the night before they should sail, he went to him and promised, that the next day he would put the device in practice, for he had got such a forcible poison as the very smell thereof should procure sudden death. … Egistus fearing that delay might breed danger, and willing that the grass should not be cut from under his feet, taking bag and baggage, with the help of Franion, conveyed himself and his men out of a postern gate of the city. …

… seeing that the Sicilians without taking their leave were fled away by night, the Bohemians feared some treason, and the king thought that without question his suspicion was true, seeing his cup-bearer had betrayed the sum of his secret pretence; whereupon he began to imagine that Franion and his wife Bellaria had conspired with Egistus, and that the fervent affection she bear him was the only means of his secret departure, in so much that, incensed with rage, he commanded that his wife should be carried to straight prison until they heard further of his pleasure.

The guard, unwilling to lay their hands on such a virtuous princess and yet fearing the king's fury, went very sorrowfully to fulfil their charge. Coming to the Queen's lodging, they found her playing with her young son, Garinter, unto whom with tears doing the message, Bellaria, astonished at such a hard censure and finding her clear conscience a sure advocate to plead in her case, went to the prison most willingly, where with sighs and tears she passed away the time till she might come to her trial.

But Pandosto, whose reason was suppressed with rage and whose unbridled folly was incensed with fury, seeing Franion had betrayed his secrets and that Egistus might well be railed on but not revenged, determined to wreak all his wrath on poor Bellaria. He therefore caused a general proclamation to be made through all his realm that the Queen and Egistus had, by the help of Franion, not only committed most incestuous adultery but also had conspired the king's death, whereupon the traitor Franion was fled away with Egistus and Bellaria was most justly imprisoned. This proclamation being once blazed through the country, although the virtuous disposition of the Queen did half discredit the contents, yet the sudden and speedy passage of Egistus and the secret departure of Franion induced them (the circumstances thoroughly considered) to think that both the proclamation was true and the king greatly injured; yet they pitied her case, as sorrowful that so good a lady should be crossed with such adverse Fortune.

… But a curst cow hath oft times short horns and a willing mind but a weak arm, for Pandosto, although he felt that revenge was a spur to war and that envy always proffereth steel, yet he saw that Egistus was not only of great puissance and prowess to withstand him but also had many kings of his alliance to aid him if need should serve, for he married to the Emperor's daughter of Russia. ...

... Bellaria continuing still in prison and hearing the contents of the proclamation ... would gladly have come to her answer. ...

But Pandosto was so enflamed with rage, and infected with jealousy, as he would not vouchsafe to hear her nor admit any just excuse. ... As thus she lay crossed with calamities (a great cause to increase her grief) she found herself quick with child, which as soon as she felt stir in her body she burst forth into bitter tears, exclaiming against Fortune in these terms:

'Alas, Bellaria, how infortunate art thou because fortunate. Better hadst thou been born a beggar than a prince, so shouldest thou have bridled Fortune with want, where now she sporteth herself with thy plenty. ... Thou art a princess, Bellaria, and yet a prisoner, born to the one by descent, assigned to the other by despite, accused without cause and therefore oughtest to die without care, for Patience is a shield against Fortune, and a guiltless mind yieldeth not to sorrow. Ah, but Infamy galleth unto death and liveth after death; Report is plumed with Time's feathers and Envie oftentimes soundeth Fame's trumpet; thy suspected adultery shall fly in the air and thy known virtues shall lie hid in the earth; one mole staineth a whole face, and what is once spotted with infamy can hardly be worn out with time. ...'

... The jailor pitying these her heavy passions, thinking that if the king knew she were with child he would somewhat appease his fury and release her from prison, went in all haste and certified Pandosto what the effect of Bellaria's complaint was, who no sooner heard the jailor say she was with child but as one possessed with a frenzy he rose up in a rage, swearing that she and the bastard brat she was withal should die if the gods themselves said no, thinking assuredly by computation of time that Egistus and not he was father to the child.

That suspicious thought galled afresh this half healed sore in so much as he could take no rest until he might mitigate his choler with a just revenge, which happened presently after. For Bellaria was brought to bed of a fair and beautiful daughter, which no sooner Pandosto heard, but he determined that both Bellaria and the young infant should be burnt with fire.

His nobles, hearing of the king's cruel sentence, sought by persuasions to divert him from this bloody determination, laying before his face the innocency of the child and virtuous disposition of his wife, how she had continually loved and honoured him so tenderly that without due proof he could not nor ought not to a-peach her of that crime. And if she had faulted, yet it were more honourable to pardon with mercy than to punish with extremity, and more kingly to be commended of pity than accused of rigour. And as for the child, if he should punish it for the mother's offence, it were to strive against nature and justice, and that unnatural actions do more offend the gods than men, how causeless cruelty nor innocent blood never scapes without revenge.

... Yet at last (seeing his noble men were importunate upon him) he was content to spare the child's life and yet to put it to a worser death. For he found out this device, that seeing (as he thought) it came by Fortune, so he would commit it to the charge of Fortune, and therefore he caused a little cock-boat to be provided, wherein he meant to put the babe and then send it to the mercy of the seas and the destinies.

From this his peers in no wise could persuade him, but that he sent presently two of his guard to fetch the child ... Bellaria no sooner heard the rigorous resolution of her merciless husband but she fell down in a swoon so that all thought she had been dead, yet at last being come to her self, she cried and screeched out in this wise:

'Alas, sweet infortunate babe, scarce born before envied by Fortune ... And shalt thou, sweet babe, be committed to Fortune when thou art already spited by Fortune? Shall the seas be thy harbour and the hard boat thy cradle? Shalt thou have the whistling winds for thy lullaby and the salt sea foam instead of sweet milk? Alas what destinies would assign such hard hap? What father would be so cruel? Or what gods will not revenge such rigour? Let me kiss thy lips (sweet infant) and wet they tender cheeks with my tears and put this chain about thy little neck, that if Fortune save thee, it may help to succour thee. ...'

Such and so great was her grief, that her vital spirits being suppressed with sorrow, she fell down in a trance, having her senses so sotted with care that after she was revived yet she lost her memory and lay for a great time without moving as one in a trance. The guard left her in this perplexity and carried the child to the king, who quite devoid of pity commanded that without delay it should be put in the boat, having neither sail nor rudder to guide it, and so to be carried into the midst of the sea, and there left to the wind and wave as the destinies please to appoint.

[The sailors make a cabin of green branches to protect the child from the weather, tow the boat out to sea, and set it adrift, where-upon] there arose a mighty tempest, which tossed the little boat so vehemently in the waves, that the shipmen thought it could not long continue without sinking, yea the storm grew so great that with much labour and peril they got to the shore.

... [Bellaria is brought to trial. She tells her husband] her virtuous life had been ever such as no spot of suspicion could ever stain. And if she had born a friendly countenance to Egistus, it was in respect he was his friend and not for any lusting affection; therefore if she were condemned without any further proof it was rigour and not law.

The noble men which sat in judgement said that Bellaria spake reason and entreated the king that the accuser might be openly examined and sworn, and if then the evidence were such as the jury might find her guilty (for seeing she was a prince she ought to be tried by her peers), then let her have such a punishment as the extremity of the law will assign to such malefactors. The king presently made answer that in this case he might, and would, dispense with the law, and that the jury being once panelled, they should take his word for sufficient evidence, otherwise he would make the proudest of them repent it. ... Bellaria, whose life then hung in the balance, fearing more perpetual infamy than momentary death, told the king if his fury might stand for a law that it were vain to have the jury yield their verdict, and therefore she fell down upon her knees and desired the king that for the love he bare to his young son Garinter, whom she brought into the world, that he would grant her request, which was this, that it would please his majesty to send six of his noble men whom he best trusted to the Isle of Delphos, there to enquire of the Oracle of Apollo whether she had committed adultery with Egistus or conspired to poison with Franion. ... The request was so reasonable that Pandosto could not for shame deny it. ... He therefore agreed ... and in the mean season, he commanded that his wife should be kept in close prison.

... [The six nobles] willing to fulfil the king's command, and desirous to see the situation and custom of the island, dispatched their affairs with as much speed as might be and embarked themselves to this voyage. ... Within three weeks they arrived at Delphos, where they were no sooner set on land, but with great devotion they went to the temple of Apollo and there, offering sacrifice to the God and gifts to the priest, as the custom was, they humbly craved an answer of their demand. They had not long kneeled at the altar but Apollo with a loud voice said, 'Bohemians, what you find behind the altar take and depart'. They forthwith obeying the Oracle found a scroll of parchment, wherein was written these words in letters of gold:

The Oracle

Suspicion is no proof, jealousy is an unequal judge, Bellaria is chaste, Egistus blameless, Franion a true subject, Pandosto treacherous, his babe an innocent, and the king shall live without an heir if that which is lost be not found.

[The nobles make good speed back to Sicily. Bellaria is brought 'as prisoner' to the Judgement Hall to hear the oracle. Before it is opened, she speaks:] 'If the divine powers be privy to human actions (as no doubt they are) I hope my patience shall make Fortune blush and my unspotted life shall stain spiteful discredit. For although lying report hath sought to a-peach mine honour and suspicion hath intended to soil my credit with infamy, yet where virtue keepeth the fort, report and suspicion may assail but never sack. How I have led my life before Egistus' coming, I appeal Pandosto to the gods and to thy conscience. What hath past betwixt him and me, the gods only know and I hope will presently reveal. That I love Egistus I cannot deny, that I honoured him I shame not to confess. To the one I was forced by his virtues, to the other to his dignities. But as touching lascivious lust, I say Egistus is honest and hope myself to be found without spot. For Franion, I can neither accuse him nor excuse him, for I was not privy to his departure. And that this is true which I have here rehearsed, I refer myself to the divine oracle.

[The oracle is read] which after the commons had heard, they gave a great shout, rejoicing and clapping their hands that the Queen was clear of that false accusation; but the king, whose conscience was a witness against him of his witless fury and false suspected jealousy, was so ashamed of his rash folly that he entreated his nobles to persuade Bellaria to forgive and forget those injuries, promising not only to show himself a loyal and loving husband but also to reconcile himself to Egistus and Franion … As thus he was relating the whole matter, there was word brought him that his young son Garinter was suddenly dead, which news so soon as Bellaria heard, surcharged before with extreme joy and now suppressed with heavy sorrow, her vital spirits were so stopped that she fell down presently dead and could never be revived.

[Pandosto, filled with remorse, attempts to kill himself. He builds a tomb for his wife and son, with an epitaph pronouncing his guilt.] Pandosto would once a day repair to the tomb and there with watery plaints bewail his misfortune, coveting no other companion but sorrow, nor no other harmony but repentance.

[Meanwhile, the baby's boat is washed up on the shores of Sicily. A poor shepherd looking for his lost sheep] fearing either that the wolves or eagles had undone him (for he was so poor as a sheep was half his substance) wandered down toward the sea cliffs to see if perchance the sheep was browsing on the sea ivy … he heard a child cry, but knowing there was no house near, he thought he had mistaken the sound and that it was the bleating of his sheep. Whereupon looking more narrowly, as he cast his eye to the sea, he spied a little boat, from whence as he attentively listened, he might hear the cry to come … At last he went to the shore, and wading to the boat, as he looked in, he saw the little babe lying all alone, ready to die for hunger and cold, wrapped in a mantle of scarlet, richly embroidered with gold and having a chain about the neck. [At first he decides to take the baby to the king, but picking it up he discovers a purse full of gold] what will not the greedy desire of gold cause a man to do? So that he was resolved in himself to foster the child. … and secretly as he could, went by a byway to his house, lest any of his neighbours should perceive his carriage. [His wife, Mopsa, assumes the child is his bastard and picks up a cudgel, but he tells her] if she can hold her peace they were made for ever.

[The gold, and Mopsa's childlessness, make her happy to bring up the baby, who they call Fawnia. Later they use some of the gold to buy their own farm. Fawnia grows into an exceptionally beautiful girl and a diligent shepherdess. By the age of 16, wearing a garland of flowers rather than any other protection from the sun] she seemed to be the goddess Flora herself for beauty.

… [Egistus has a son, Dorastus, who is now twenty. His father wishes to marry him to a Danish princess, but he has no desire to wed. One day, he is out hunting and comes across a 'meeting of all the farmers' daughters in Sicily, whither Fawnia was also bidden as the mistress of the feast'. He talks to her. She answers him] with such modest reverence and sharpness of wit, that Dorastus thought her outward beauty was but a counterfeit to darken her inward qualities, wondering how so courtly behaviour could be found in so simple a cottage.

[They fall in love and each tries to get the other out of their thoughts. Greene devotes several pages to these struggles. Eventually Dorastus comes to think 'if her birth were answerable to her wit and beauty, she were a fit mate for the most famous prince in the world', but Fawnia berates herself 'why dost thou gaze against the sun, or catch at the wind?' Dorastus disguises himself in shepherd's rags to visit her and reflects that the gods themselves] have sometime earthly thoughts: Neptune became a ram, Jupiter a bull, Apollo a shepherd.

[Eventually he persuades Fawnia to run away with him and promises to make careful preparations. He keeps visiting Fawnia in disguise so that the neighbours become suspicious and tell the old Shepherd, who talks to his wife. They decide to tell the king how they found the baby. Dorastus enlists the help of an old servant, Capnio to help organise the elopement. Dorastus and Fawnia succeed in getting on board a ship. Later Capnio intercepts the shepherd 'trudging as fast as he could with a little coffer under his arm' who tells him that he is going to see the king. In order to prevent this, Capnio tells him that the king has gone aboard ship. When they get to the seaside the mariners take the shepherd forcibly aboard the prince's ship, which sails for Italy. Meanwhile Egistus fears that Dorastus has been killed by a wild animal while out hunting. He scours the kingdom. Two fishermen report that they had seen Dorastus, Fawnia, Capnio and the shepherd going aboard the ship.]

[Dorastus's and Fawnia's ship is caught in a terrible storm but arrives on the 'coast of Bohemia'. They land intending to marry, but news of her beauty spreads through the country. 'Pandosto, who then being about the age of fifty had notwithstanding young and fresh affections' desires to see her. He arrests them. Dorastus explains that he is Meleagrus, a gentleman of Trapalonia and that his intended wife is an Italian from Padua, whose friends had not consented to the marriage. Pandosto does not believe him; the woman is so beautiful she is fitter for a prince rather than a mere knight. He has Dorastus thrown into prison. He is much taken with Fawnia and makes advances to her. She replies] 'I had rather be Meleagrus wife and a beggar, than live in plenty and be Pandosto's concubine'.

[Eventually Egistus's ambassadors arrive. They demand that Dorastus be released and Fawnia, Capnio, and the Shepherd executed. Pandosto rages against Fawnia, 'How durst though, being a beggar, to match with a prince? By thy alluring looks, to enchant the son of a king to leave his own country to fulfil thy disordinate lusts? O despiteful mind, a proud heart in a beggar is not unlike to a great fire in a small cottage, which warmeth not the house, but burneth it'. The fear of death causes the Shepherd to tell his story. He produces the 'mantle of scarlet', the chain and jewels. Pandosto eagerly checks the details of the story, and] suddenly leapt from his seat and kissed Fawnia, wetting her tender cheeks with his tears and crying, 'My daughter Fawnia, ah, sweet Fawnia, I am thy father, Fawnia'.

Fawnia was not more joyful that she had found such a father than Dorastus was glad he should get such a wife. The ambassadors rejoiced that their young prince had made such a choice, that these kingdoms which through enmity had long time been dissevered should now through perpetual amity be united and reconciled. The citizens and subjects of Bohemia (hearing that the king had found again his daughter, which was supposed dead, joyful that there was an heir apparent to his kingdom) made bonfires and shows throughout the city.

[After eighteen days of celebration, the shepherd is knighted. Pandosto and the young couple travel to Sicily where Egistus welcomes them and the marriage is celebrated, after which] Pandosto, calling to mind how first he betrayed his friend Egistus, how his jealousy was the cause of Bellaria's death, that contrary to the law of nature he had lusted after his own daughter, moved with these desperate thoughts, he fell into a melancholy fit, and to close up the comedy with a tragical stratagem, he slew himself. [Dorastus and Fawnia accompany the corpse to Bohemia, where] Dorastus ended his days in contented quiet.

Sicily and Bohemia

Greene is following a well-established tradition in placing the pastoral section of his story in Sicily. The Greek poet Theocritus, who invented the eclogue or pastoral in the third century BC, had set his *Idylls* there, and Sicily, not Bohemia, has been the natural literary home for wise shepherds ever since. Bohemia is a country that corresponds to the modern Czech Republic. It has no sea coast. It is usually assumed that in reversing the countries, Shakespeare made a mistake or was ignorant of European geography, although Greene too refers to the 'coast of Bohemia', perhaps to reinforce the mythic nature of his tale.

The Kingdom of Bohemia, like much of the rest of Europe at that time, had been acquired by the Hapsburg family through marriage – in this case by the marriage of the German Emperor Ferdinand I to Anne of Bohemia. Its king was now their grandson Rudolph II, who, like his father Maximilian II, was also Holy Roman Emperor. He had made Prague his principal residence, but his empire included Dalmatia and Croatia, and thus a coastline to the Adriatic. His mother, Maria, was a daughter of the Emperor Charles V, also a Hapsburg, and King of Spain. Through inheritance from the house of Aragon, the kingdom of Sicily now belonged to the descendants of Charles's son Philip II. Actual landholdings in early seventeenth-century Europe were thus no more mixed up politically and nationally than the countries in Shakespeare's play. Fortuitously, sixteenth-century maps of the kingdom of Bohemia tend to show a country not unlike Sicily in shape, entirely surrounded by a ring of mountains, almost a little island in the middle of Europe. Shakespeare's reversal and intermingling of the two countries thus begins to look like a deliberate choice.

Bohemia had had a turbulent religious history, and for the sake of peace, Bohemians had been granted an unusual amount of religious freedom. Uniquely, therefore, the 1552 map of Bohemia by Sebastian Münster marks the dominant religion (Catholic or Protestant) of each major town. Bohemia was itself an elective monarchy. Its king was also entitled to two votes in the election of the Holy Roman Emperor. Whoever ruled Bohemia therefore held a significant balance of power in Europe.

By the early years of the seventeenth century, the reclusive King and Emperor Rudolph was childless, aging and probably suffering from mental illness. In July 1609, he had granted a Letter of Majesty, confirming freedom of conscience in the Bohemian lands, but almost immediately he began to dispute its terms. His cousin Arch-Duke Leopold V of Austria mobilised a mercenary army, ostensibly on his behalf, but this was unpaid and ransacked its way through Bavaria to Prague. The Bohemian nobles appealed for help to Rudolph's brother and heir, Matthias, King of Hungary, who marched on Prague and, on 11 November 1611, forced Rudolph to abdicate. He died the following year.

The crisis had coincided with the question of succession in the German territories of Juliers-Cleves, claimed by two Protestant princes who agreed to rule jointly until a compromise could be reached. Rudolph, however, was determined to prevent these strategically situated states falling into Protestant hands. Henri IV of France had been supporting the Protestant claimants but was assassinated in May 1610, an event which caused great alarm and fear in the English royal households. By the time Simon Forman saw a performance of *The Winter's Tale* at the Globe in May 1611, the future of Bohemia was an international problem and a number of countries were mobilised for war.

While Henry, Prince of Wales was always keen to give military support to the Protestant cause in Europe, his father James I was determined to maintain peace, and to this end was busy negotiating a balance of Catholic and Protestant marriage alliances for his three children. There were several contenders for the kingship of Bohemia, including the Catholic Duke of Savoy. On 3 April 1611 Salisbury, James I's first minister, wrote to Ralph Winwood (then English Resident, or ambassador, at the Hague, and James's chief negotiator for peace in Europe), briefing him that the Duke of Savoy's ambassador had visited the English court to explain Savoy's taking up arms in the Juliers dispute: 'he then declared himself, that he had in charge to propose a double match between the Prince of Savoy his Master's eldest son and the king our master's daughter, and between the daughter of Savoy and the Prince of Wales'. Clearly this double match was not going to be acceptable, although the dangling prospect of political alliance was an important diplomatic tool for as long as the royal children remained unmarried. Equally clearly, the religious affiliation of prospective suitors was a bone of contention within the royal family itself, with Anne of Denmark, James's queen, favouring the Catholic side.

Following Greene, the play elides historical periods, referring both to the Emperor of Russia (Egistus's father-in-law, but Hermione's father), and the classical oracle at Delphos (which is not unusually equated with the Island of Kythera in both Greene and Shakespeare). But Shakespeare also introduces a very English set of shepherds and music-making into this strange vision of central Europe. The joke about the Shepherd's son becoming a gentleman born before his father makes a contemporary English reference, since James's desperate need to raise money had resulted in large-scale selling of honours. This joke is also personal to Shakespeare, since, somewhat to the consternation of the College of Arms, who did not approve of a mere player becoming a gentleman, he had bought the right to a coat of arms for his father, which technically made him too a 'gentleman born'.

Shakespeare's mixing of geographical, literary and historical attributes thus dissolves and elides countries that might be seen as standing on opposite sides of longstanding conflicts. In bringing all to joyful conclusion in marriage, it could therefore be read by contemporaries as reflecting James's attempts to bring peace and religious unity to Europe. The dream of political accord is apparent in the first scene between Archidamus and Camillo, the two kings' trusted servants, and also in King Polixenes's description of his and Leontes's childhoods (I.ii.63–88). Their boyhood years together are described as some prelapsarian Eden, a time of peace and friendship in which they were inseparable. Hermione jokes that they have 'tripped' since, and of course Leontes's suspicion of her adultery with his friend results in schism, death and threats of murder. The return of Perdita to Sicily, however, is said to bring back spring to a wintry kingdom, and is Shakespeare's version of the opening of Virgil's *Eclogue* IV. This poem's first line appeals to the Sicilian muses and goes on to celebrate return, rebirth and a new age:

> Iam redit et Virgo, redeunt Saturnia regna
> Iam nova progenies caelo demittitur alto
> Tu modo nascenti puero, quo ferrea primum
> Desinet ac toto surget gens aurea mundo,
> Casta fave Lucina: tuus iam regnat Apollo
> (ll.6–10)

'Now the Virgin (i.e. Astraea, goddess of Justice) returns, the reign of Saturn returns; now a new generation descends from heaven on high. Only do thou, pure Lucina, smile on the birth of the child, under whom the iron brood shall first cease, and a golden race spring up throughout the world. Thine own Apollo now is king' (tr. H. Rushton Fairclough, Loeb Classical Library 1950).

Virgil is celebrating a new golden age under the Emperor Caesar Augustus. No one who saw *The Winter's Tale* in performance at court would have been unaware that James I had been modelling himself on this emperor. Ben Jonson's verses performed along the processional route for his coronation in March 1604 had included this same quotation, referring to James repeatedly as Emperor and as Caesar Augustus (Jonson, *Works*, 1616). But some Englishmen were suspicious of the aspirations of their Scottish king and his tendency to refer to himself as a god. Parliament was reluctant to grant him money and had refused his attempt to unite England and Scotland, partly because of what they saw as a threat to their liberty of speech. Likewise, to a sixteenth-century classically educated audience, Sicily, in the form of the court of Dionysius (c. 430–367 BC) at Syracuse, was a byword for tyranny, and this knowledge would have echoed in Paulina's repeated accusations that the Sicilian Leontes is a tyrant. There was a real question about where the absolutist tendencies of the house of Stuart would take the English monarchy, which underlies all of Shakespeare's Jacobean plays.

Shakespeare's mixed genre

In his *Arte of English Poesie* (1589), George Puttenham explained that far from being the simplest, most ancient of forms, as one might suppose from the fact that it is populated by simple shepherds, the eclogue or pastoral is not intended 'to counterfeit or represent the rustical manner of loves and communication, but under the veil of homely persons, and in rude speeches to insinuate and glance at greater matters' (Book 1, chap. xviii). In other words, it lends itself as a cover for talking about politics. Pastoral, he says, mixes the older forms of tragedy and comedy, in order to 'contain and enform moral discipline, for the amendment of man's behaviour'.

Following the rediscovery of the *Aethiopian History* by the Greek poet Heliodorus in the second half of the sixteenth century, romance, which likewise involves forays into a landscape, had become an immensely popular form of prose fiction throughout Europe, aimed at the middling sort of reader, and acceptable to English Protestants because of its emphasis on providence. The central character in these narratives was no longer the wandering knight of the medieval chivalric romances but a long-suffering, patient heroine in love. Robert Greene's first experiment in the genre was *Mamillia* (1580), whose name seems to have been borrowed by Shakespeare for Leontes's son – another of the strange reversals in the play.

It is often said that in *The Winter's Tale*, Shakespeare, in his old age, was adopting a new form of pastoral romance from a rising star, John Fletcher, whose pastoral *The Faithful Shepherdess* (based on *Il Pastor*

Fido, a pastoral tragiccomedy by Giovanni Battista Guarini), had been performed by Shakespeare's company in 1608. Nothing could be further from the truth. Shakespeare was not old. He was in his mid forties, in the prime of life and the height of his powers. He had explored tragicomedy, romance and pastoral on numerous occasions previously, and Fletcher's play had been far from successful.

The firm division of Shakespeare's plays into histories, comedies and tragedies in the first Folio of his works, printed posthumously, has been misleading. All of Shakespeare's plays in fact mix comedy and tragedy. As early as *The Comedy of Errors* (c. 1589), he had combined elements of romance – long lost children, a quest, and suggestions of magic arts – with the urban and politically motivated 'tragical comedy' form (derived from the play *Amphitruo* by the Roman poet Plautus, and exemplified in England by Richard Edwards's play *Damon and Pythias*, 1564–5).

Tragicomedy is often characterised as a V: a descent into hell and a climb back out. If one were to draw a topographical diagram of the structure of *The Winter's Tale*, it would consist of a fairly smooth slide down into the depths of misery throughout the first three acts of the play, bottoming out on the seacoast of Bohemia as Antigonus abandons the baby. We, the audience, know where she is, however. She is not lost to us and at that point, only halfway through the play, we may be sure that the story will follow her. Things immediately get better since she is found by someone who seems prepared to look after her. This and the death of Antigonus offstage, comically recounted by the clown, refocus our attention. We are no longer allowed to dwell on 'things dying'.

After Time's intervention, we appear to be in another kind of world altogether. This has caused commentators and directors of the play enormous anxiety, and many people have tried to even out the contrasts. The climb back up from the bottom of the V, however, is not nearly so smooth as the descent. The music and pastoral setting recall the story of Orpheus who could tame wild animals by playing his lute, but that story tells us that there is death too in Arcadia (*Et in Arcadia ego*). Orpheus lost his wife Euridyce twice to death: first through a snake bite, and then, in trying to rescue her from hell, he lost her forever because he broke the injunction not to look back at her (Ovid, *Metamorphoses*, X). There are dangers lurking also in the Arcadian Bohemia of this play. After every step up, there is a fall back, as if the turning of Time's glass also involves a spinning of Fortune's wheel. Some of those setbacks involve threats of death that would in reality be every bit as frightening as those in the first half of the play. Some- times such threats are terrifying for the character but hilarious for us, as when Autolycus, pretending to be a courtier, threatens the Shepherd's son with death by a thousand wasp stings (IV.iv.785). Laughter and tears, horror and humour, don't just alternate, they mingle.

As in *Cymbeline*, the audience is in possession of all the information (save one crucial fact) throughout the second half. But in *Cymbeline*, the process whereby the characters are told what we already know is played out in front of us. This makes for a very long final scene, which is quite tedious to read, although it can be immense fun in perform- ance as each character suddenly realises their part in the jigsaw. In *The Winter's Tale*, by contrast, the things that we already know are played out offstage. Act V opens with the return to Sicily and the reintegration of the characters from the Sicilian and Bohemian scenes of the play. The characters in that scene variously experience joy, regret, fear, terror and anger but these intense emotions are played out, for us, against the backdrop of our knowledge that Florizel's shepherdess is Leontes's lost daughter. It is an irony that allows us to acknowledge the characters' feelings while keeping safely distant. We are more amused than fear- ful, and more intrigued than either, wondering how it is all going to turn out, but reasonably confident that it will turn out well.

That confidence is rewarded in V.ii when the gentlemen tell us that the truth has been discovered. Oddly, their amazement at the event increases our sense of the verisimilitude of this frankly impossible tale. These three Gentlemen are on the edges of the story, and not at all emotionally involved on a personal level. As the Third Gentleman says, it 'angled for mine eyes – caught the water, though not the fish' (V.ii.82–3). They have experienced exactly the pleasurable sorrow that we as readers and spectators feel when we consume works of fiction: the experience that Shakespeare is saving up for us for the final scene.

Names and the quality of Hermes

As with *Cymbeline*, the names in this play are either functional (Old Shepherd, Clown, Lord) or meaningful. All are different from those of the corresponding characters in *Pandosto*. Most of the meaningful

names have Latin, or occasionally Greek roots. Perdita (Lat. 'lost')
and Florizel (cf. Lat. *floreus*, 'made of flowers') are self explanatory,
but a Don Florisel de Niquea is the eponymous hero of the second of
Feliciano de Silva's three additional volumes to the famous romance
the *Amadis de Gaule* (1532). Florizel's pseudonym, Doricles, is from
Doric, signifying the most ancient and therefore most rustic of the
ancient Greek tribes, and invariably denotes simplicity or rusticity
whether in music, architecture or poetry. The name is accordingly
also used for a young prince of Arcadia in George Chapman's popular satirical comedy, *The Blind Beggar of Alexandria* (1595/6), a play
advertised on its title page (1598) as containing 'variable humours in
disguised shapes'. The name Leontes, from Latin *leo natus* 'lion born',
bears striking similarity with Posthumus Leonatus, the young lead
male part in *Cymbeline*, who likewise becomes obsessed with the idea
that his wife is unfaithful. The lion, the king of beasts, is of course
commonly associated with kingship, but in this play may be just one
more example of Shakespeare's deliberate mingling and reversal of
Sicily and Bohemia, since a lion with forked tail was the distinctive
emblem of Bohemia. Michael Bristol ('In Search of the Bear', p. 156)
points out that Leo is the zodiacal sign associated with high summer
and that Polixenes suggests 'polus' north star and constancy. Again,
the opposites are true in the play since Leontes is king of a wintry
court and Polixenes flies, abandoning Hermione to her fate.

More intriguing is the play's connection with the Roman god
Mercury, known in Greek as Hermes. Here too there is a Sicilian/
Bohemian mixture which unites two seemingly disparate characters:
Hermione and Autolycus. Known as the messenger of the gods and
the guide of souls, Mercury/Hermes is associated with fertility but
often represented by a mere stone, a herm, perhaps carved with a human
head and a phallus. An ancient connection with the stones of road-
side cairns also made him the patron of travellers, merchants and
thieves, while the myth that he had invented the lyre, a small Greek
harp, combined with his role as messenger, meant that he became
associated with oratory and later with literature. His son Autolycus
was the grandfather of the wily Greek hero Odysseus, and described
by Homer as 'the most accomplished thief and liar of his day' (*Odyssey*,
19.394). In this play, Autolycus has the gift of the gab, necessary for
the con artist, thief and ballad monger. He travels the country, 'haunts
wakes, fairs and bair-baitings' (ll. 100–1). Hermione, by contrast, displays

Hermes's gift for oratory and also his stone-like qualities, both in her still dignity at her trial in III.ii and also as the statue in V.iii.

There is also a possible mercurial link between Autolycus and Camillo. In *De Lingua Latina* (7.3.34) by the Roman writer Varro (who also wrote a famous treatise on agriculture), a Camillus is associated with a Hermes cult in the Samothracian region of Greece. Autolycus claims he was nearly the first person to discover the truth of the shepherdess's birth because he brought the Old Shepherd and his son aboard Florizel and Perdita's ship for his personal gain, thus doing good against his nature (V.ii.112–22, cf. IV.iv.832–43). Camillo likewise, for personal reasons, arranges for all the characters to travel to Sicily, thus doing good as a side effect to his own desires (IV.iv.543–54, 663–8).

The Triumph of Time

The title page of Greene's *Pandosto* quotes the proverb *Temporis filia veritas* (Truth is the daughter of Time) and advertises the story as a 'pleasant history' that will be 'profitable' to both youth and age, demonstrating 'that although by the means of sinister Fortune Truth may be concealed, yet by Time in spite of Fortune it is most manifestly revealed'. Greene does not introduce Time as a character in this story, but uses the classical connection between Chronos (time) and Kairos (opportunity, occasion), to invoke the concept of Fortune, which is the prime motivating force in his story.

The Roman practice of military triumphal procession had been taken up across Europe during the Renaissance as an expression of power and magnificence, allowing a ruler to show himself to his people. It was the fourteenth-century Italian poet Francis Petrarch who turned the custom into an allegorical art form. His *Trionfi* is a series of six poems describing the triumphs of Love, Chastity, Death, Fame, Time, and Eternity. Each personification in turn is shown victorious over the one before. This series was perhaps even more famous during his lifetime than his sonnets, the poems for which he is chiefly remembered today, and circulated widely. All over Europe, painters, potters, tapestry weavers, furniture makers, and silver smiths turned out household artefacts decorated with allegorical images inspired by this series. The first complete translation into English was made by the statesman and diplomat Henry Parker, Lord Morley and printed some time in the early 1550s.

Unlike Greene, Shakespeare introduces Time as a character, who appears, conventionally equipped with scythe and hourglass. In mechanical terms, the turning of that glass should merely measure what is to come, which here would be the second of the conventional 'two hours' traffic' of the stage (*Romeo and Juliet*, Prologue 12). This speech, however, designated as 'Chorus' in the F text, has a number of different functions. In narrative terms, it links together the two parts of the story, set as they are in different countries, at different periods and with a largely different set of characters. The turning of Time's glass leaps over the years needed for the baby to grow into a young woman. But, paradoxically, turning an hourglass causes the sand in it to trickle back the way it has come. So Time's action is also a metaphor for the process whereby the tragic events of the first part of the play will be at least partly reversed. The opening lines of his speech accordingly contain a series of reversals and opposites but these also combine with the metre to imitate the slightly limping, tick-tock rhythm of a mechanical clock:

```
x         x      x      x      x
I that please some, try all; both joy and terror
   x       x        x        x       x
Of good and bad, that makes and unfolds error
                              (IV.i.1–2)
```

Mechanical clocks of this period are powered by the gravitational pull of a weight, wound up (by hand) on a string on a daily basis. The descent of this weight is regulated by an escapement mechanism, which releases power in short, regular bursts. It is the escapement that produces the characteristic tick tock sound. The circular movement of the human hand converts to the vertical movement of the weight, which turns the cogs, which in turn causes cyclical movement of the hands, or sometimes planets and zodiacal signs, on the clock face. Shakespeare integrates such contrasting movements into the structure of the entire play. Time and events drag, rush, jump forwards, slide back, run in cycles or in parallel. Aural images and stage pictures shake hands 'as over a vast' (I.i.30), connecting characters and events in strange reversals across the play and between the courts and countries of Sicily and Bohemia. As Time jumps forwards in this play, the seasons move backwards. The first half of the play has been locked securely in winter. The sheep-shearing festival is the height of midsummer. But when Perdita returns with her future husband to Sicily and meets her father for the first time, although he as yet knows not who she is, he greets the son of his lost friend with the words 'Welcome hither, / As is the spring to th'earth' (V.i.150–1).

Shakespeare also uses Time's speech triumphantly to draw attention to one of the greatest 'errors' in literary theory: the requirement to obey the 'unities' of time and place, both of which are broken in this play. Commentators of the sixteenth century had mistakenly derived this rule from Aristotle's *Art of Poetry*, although Aristotle in fact demands merely a unity of action. The word 'error' might also hark back half a lifetime to *The Comedy of Errors*, which story covers many years and wide geographical spaces, but which Shakespeare, following the first of his two sources (Plautus's *Menaechmi*), begins and completes in the same town within a single day. Shakespeare's entire career was one of conscious experimentation with literary and dramatic forms but Time's speech is perhaps the only overt piece of literary theory in all his plays:

> Impute it not a crime
> To me or my swift passage that I slide
> O'er sixteen years and leave the growth untried
> Of that wide gap, since it is in my power
> To o'erthrow law, and in one self-born hour
> To plant and o'erwhelm custom.
>
> (IV.i.4–9)

Despite the warning, those brought up on the notion of the 'three unities' of time, place and action have been (misguidedly) imputing the play's structure a crime ever since. But the absolute enormity of what Time is saying here is frightening. Unlike Greene's revelation of truth, time in this play is not a moral force, merely a process for change. The monstrousness of being 'self-born', the ability to overthrow laws, and both to instil new customs and overthrow old ones, is a description of tyrannical, arbitrary, autocratic rule that might appal anyone committed to stable government under a monarch ruling with the advice of both council and Parliament.

Time may therefore appear to be a straightforward allegorical character, complete with all his usual attributes, speaking in what sounds initially like archaic rhyming couplets, which help to characterise his age and ancient identity, but his actual effect is far from straightforward. As he turns his glass, promising a change of place (to Bohemia), and of time (sixteen years later), his language changes. He drops his assertive organising of events. The tone becomes playful, suggestive rather than determining; he tantalises us with mention of Perdita, but draws back 'What of her ensues / I list not prophesy' (IV.i.25–6). It is timing, after all, that makes both an accomplished storyteller and a great actor. A storyteller's success lies less in revealing 'truth' than in creating suspense, or anticipation and, once we are captivated by the experience, sometimes in telling us what we know already. All of these techniques are put to use in the final act of the play.

Time's speech also does something particularly interesting with its verse. Although the whole speech is tied together in rhyming couplets, it incorporates three different types of rhythm. After the strongly onomatopoeic rhythm of the first couplet, where the metre emphasises the reversals expressed in the words, it reverts to a generalised, though still highly regular, iambic pentameter (ll. 3–16). Then, 'leaving' Leontes after the gesture of turning the glass, it slides into syllabic verse (ll. 17–32): these lines are still completely regular with ten (occasionally eleven) syllables, but the syllables are no longer alternately accented. By the time Shakespeare was writing, syllabic verse was deemed to be old-fashioned, although the most popular and most frequently reprinted poetry miscellanies of the sixteenth and early seventeenth centuries – such as Richard Edwards's collection, *The Paradise of Dainty Devices* – consisted almost entirely of such verse. Syllabic poetry demands to be spoken according to the prose rhythm of the words. Indeed it often comes to life only when sung, for a rhythmic melody releases it from what otherwise appears to be the relentless succession of equal syllables. As Time's turning glass turns winter to high summer and romance tragedy to romantic comedy, his speech transforms from the formality of metre into the English vernacular of syllabic verse. It allows for the transition to the vernacular music of popular ballad, which characterises the second half of the play.

While it may often be assumed that the primary feature of music is differing pitch, it is in fact rhythm, which distinguishes music from mere sound. And for rhythm to be recognisable as such, it must 'keep time'. It is therefore not accidental that Shakespeare's play about time should contain an unusual amount of music, and that this is used dramaturgically, not just decoratively.

The grim first half of the play is characterised by a lack of musical sound. After Hermione's supposed death, time stops for Leontes's court, as he resorts to an unending round of visits to her tomb. The exposure of the baby, by contrast, is performed to a cacophony of thunder, storm and the raucous din of hunting horns, 'out of time and harsh' to quote Ophelia's line in the Folio text of *Hamlet* (III.i.161).

The unfolding of time is accompanied by the social performance of ballads and dances. But the restitution of Hermione in the supposed awakening of the statue is accomplished through a theatrical effect that is invariably extremely moving: words spoken over music. We now are used to film music that underscores a particular emotion, supplying a sense of tension or of surprise when few if any words are spoken, but this is rather different. Here, Paulina's musicians will be performing a piece of music that in other circumstances could stand alone as a work of art, with a musical logic and an emotional affective power of its own. It is performed as an equal partner to the dialogue between Paulina and Leontes, without setting those words or coinciding with their rhythmic or emotional peaks and troughs. Words and music simply coexist, and we in the audience listen to both simultaneously. It is perhaps the fact that they do not synchronise that allows us the space to bring a third set of emotional values and memories to the scene: our own. The music will allow us to connect with our own feelings of loss, regret and love, which will inevitably be very much more real to us than those being performed by the actors on the stage, no matter how accomplished they are. We can thereby disregard the impossibility of the events of that story and acknowledge the reality of the desires that it represents.

Silence

At the turn of the seventeenth century, there were many moralists demanding that women should be silent in public. Women's silence in this play, however, is more interesting, and more eloquent than anything those men had in mind. In performance, the visibly pregnant Hermione, probably playing with her son, is the centre of attention long before she speaks in Act I scene ii. Later, when she enters to her trial, her dignity silences the court (see Commentary pp. 29–30). In the final scene she embraces her husband, which Polixenes and Camillo interpret as a gesture of love, but she never speaks to him (see Commentary pp. 74–5). In all cases, her silent but commanding presence questions the dialogue going on around her.

Critics of the nineteenth and in some cases twentieth centuries were simply charmed, however, by what they saw as Perdita's elegant reticence. She is, of course, painfully aware that her union with Florizel will not be sanctioned by his father, and on occasion, she is embarrassed into silence because of her lack of education (IV.iv.378–91). But she feels passionately about her right to love Florizel and, after Polixenes has revealed himself and stormed out, she berates herself for not speaking:

> I was not much afeard, for once or twice
> I was about to speak, and tell him plainly
> The selfsame sun that shines upon his court
> Hides not his visage from our cottage. …
> (IV.iv.442–5)

Ironically, it is now Florizel who is silenced by the pressures of family and hierarchy, and as she becomes aware of that, it is her silent gesture that becomes eloquent: she stares at him. This eventually pricks him into speech but it takes four or five lines of antithesis and reversal before he regains his composure (IV.iv.462–6). When they arrive in Sicily, however, she is silenced by him, neither confirming nor denying the long rigmarole of lies he tells to explain their sudden arrival (V.i.137–77). Gradually her presence in the play seems to give place to Hermione, to the extent that some productions have made the same actor play both parts. But one of the reasons why this attempt to underscore the family resemblance between mother and daughter never works in practice is that it ignores the power of silence on the stage, while distracting us into wondering about the mechanics of the staging. Leontes may demand in Perdita's name to see the statue, and Paulina may tell her to intercede with her mother, but it is Perdita's silent gaze that directs our attention and imagination to the deep emotional tie between mother and daughter who have been denied knowledge of each other for so long (V.iii.41–2).

Experiencing Leontes's jealousy

Theatre is a multimedia art form which depends on aural and visual experience as well as words. Shakespeare's language frequently demands specific gestures from actors, as when Leontes observes that Hermione lifts her face to Polixenes, and takes his arm – as if she were his wife (I.ii.185). As this incident demonstrates, *The Winter's Tale* is acutely concerned with both the connection and the scope for misinterpretation in word and gesture. Shakespeare knows that gestures like words are sometimes too full of meaning and rarely unambiguous. His problem is to let us see quite unequivocally that Hermione is innocent, while also making us understand how Leontes comes to 'read' those gestures as proof of her guilt.

In performance, we and Leontes see Hermione lift her face to Polixenes at the same moment. The nature of her gesture will have been chosen by actor and director during the process of rehearsal, and is usually determined by what has already been established about her open, direct and playful character. We then hear Leontes's description of that gesture, which has been designed by Shakespeare to indicate *his* mental state. His phrase 'the neb, the bill' (i.e. snout, beak, I.ii.184) implies bestiality, not innocence. It will not tally with what we see (unless, as sometimes in modern productions, a decision has been made to show us, through lighting or other effect, that what we have seen is somehow in his head). When reading, however, we not only have to reconstruct the gesture in retrospect *after* Leontes has told us about it, but we also have to correct it without the help of any visual prompt.

The most difficult speeches to read and understand in the entire play are probably those in which Leontes tells us about his conviction that Hermione is unfaithful. Both in terms of syntax and motivation, these have caused endless difficulty. Having failed to make his old friend Polixenes stay longer in his court, Leontes has asked his dear wife to try to persuade him. She quickly gets Polixenes's agreement to stay another week but Leontes interprets her success as firm evidence of her infidelity. At what point in the dialogue of this scene, critics have asked, does Leontes suddenly become jealous? And is this suddenness not rather unbelievable, a fault in the conception and construction of the play?

That an actor should feel a character's emotion has been a central tenet of the Stanislavskian and Method approaches to acting. Edward Hall, however, who has directed a series of highly acclaimed all male productions of Shakespeare, including one of *The Winter's Tale*, has stressed that, particularly where actor and character do not even share the same gender, successful performance resides in the actor's skill in presenting that emotion to the audience so that *they* can begin to feel it (BBC Radio 4, *Start the Week*, 8 January 2007).

Shakespeare's task is to enable a large and disparate body of people, who have all walked into the theatre with different life experiences and in different moods, communally to get to a level of understanding of an extreme emotion. This emotion does not reside in one character alone. Leontes's entire family and court are caught up in his jealousy and there is no major character in the play whose life is not marred by it. This social experience of a single man's mental breakdown finds expression in the way the verse is arranged from speaker to speaker. There is a real sense of interaction in the dialogue, and also of people talking at cross purposes. The metre is shared between speakers, and almost without exception speeches begin and end on the half line.

We are therefore not just being asked to observe a character's state of mind but to experience a dynamic process in which our imaginations too have to play a part. From the very first line of the play the language of every character has included quirks and oddities, the potential for puns and word play whereby we can both see and feel what Leontes fears, while simultaneously realising that what he fears is a fiction.

Polixenes has begun the second scene with the lines:

Nine changes of the wat'ry star hath been
The shepherd's note since we have left our throne
Without a burden.

This is evidently more complex than it needs to be simply to make his excuses and leave. He is intending to be polite and courtly, but the lines, spoken in front of a woman who is heavily pregnant, are themselves pregnant with sex. Shakespeare's combination of language and stage picture here simulates familiar mental processes; we can probably all remember times when we have been prompted by a visual cue to a perhaps unconscious choice of word, sometimes with embarrassing consequences. Polixenes is king of a country, which will be characterised later in the play by that ritual celebration of rural fecundity, a sheep-shearing feast. Such feasts are the opportunity for young people to meet and do what young people tend to do at times of holiday. They are invariably accompanied by music, song and sexual banter – shepherds' 'notes' indeed. One of the 'true' ballads that the pedlar Autolycus will pick out for sale to the credulous shepherdess Mopsa tells 'how a usurer's wife was brought to bed of twenty money-bags at a burden'. He points out the verification in print, 'Here's the midwife's name to't, one Mistress Tail-Porter' – a name with suitably lewd connotations – and continues with a further pun on 'tale-porter': 'Why should I carry lies abroad?' (IV.iv.256–65). By that point in the play, however, we will have seen that Hermione's pregnancy is a phys-ical, mental and/or social burden for everyone touched by it – even Antigonus, who *carries* the resulting child to its fate, and dies in the process. The ballad in Act IV merely makes crudely explicit something established as a structural pattern in the play from its very opening.

Although she is silent throughout the initial dialogue between Polixenes and her husband, Hermione's presence and physical con-dition mean that the word 'burden' in Polixenes's language assumes a pun on pregnancy. It may not be a pun that the character intends on any level, but the collocation of 'note' and 'burden' (chorus or refrain, commonly found in ballad form), indicates that some con-nection with popular song was in Shakespeare's mind when he wrote the line. Stage picture and poetic image thus combine in a lewd interpretation – if one is that way inclined.

Close attention to the sound of his utterances, and not just the semantic meaning of what he says, shows that Leontes is conscious of the coincidence, and is already that way inclined. Shakespeare took ready-made from his source, Greene's *Pandosto*, a set of behaviours that corresponds closely not just to jealousy (which might be regarded as a normal state of mind when there is something actually to be jealous about) but to a syndrome that some modern psychiatrists call 'morbid jealousy'. This is a term used to describe an obsession with a partner's sexual infidelity through unshakeable misinterpretation of irrelevant evidence, *whether or not* the partner is unfaithful. It may present in a range of different psychiatric diagnoses, and may be accompanied with extreme and violent behaviour. Sufferers commonly feel perse-cuted, displaying a fear of being poisoned (see III.ii.15–16, 77), or that their partner is being unfaithful while they sleep, which might per-haps account for Leontes's sleeplessness at II.iii.1–4. This pathology has occasionally been termed 'Othello syndrome', although with less justification, since Othello's belief in Desdemona's infidelity derives from Iago's manipulation of the behaviour of all the characters in the play and is therefore less irrational (although equally untrue). Leontes's jealousy is blacker because he deliberately eggs her on in order to find proof of her fault, and his conclusion does not depend on the agency of any other person, as Othello's jealousy depends on Iago.

There is always a severe problem, however, with connecting modern diagnoses of diseases with people from the past, even when the disease is physical, since we are dependent on third-party observations, coloured by historical beliefs – as indeed we are when the sufferer is fictional. This difficulty is compounded, however, where the disease is psychological, since psychological diagnoses are often more contested among modern clinicians. Sigmund Freud, in *Some Neurotic Mechanisms in Jealousy, Paranoia and Homosexuality* (1922), for instance, thought that what he termed 'delusional jealousy' indicated latent homosexuality, as in 'I do not love him because she loves him'. This is an idea which has been applied to the play on a number of occasions since the 1940s. More recently, morbid jealousy has been seen as stemming from a sense of inadequacy – although it might be equally valid to deduce that any sense of inadequacy in the sufferer is the *result* of the delusional jealousy, or its underlying cause.

It is therefore dangerous to make a diagnosis of the behaviour exhibited in the play and use that to identify or construct causation in the character's past before the play begins, and for which we therefore have little or no evidence. Thus the most that can be claimed, although it is an important claim, is that Leontes exhibits a form of pathological behaviour, which is far from uncommon. This behaviour may have a range of currently unknown causes, and is a symptom rather than a diagnosis, but Leontes's delusion is not incomprehensibly unique in the way it has seemed to so many critics. In any case, it is Greene who observed the symptoms and gave them to his character, Pandosto. Shakespeare's task here has been to dramatise them, through sound and gesture as well as semantics, so as to enable audiences to understand the full force and horror of Leontes's state of mind, by experiencing it with him. Such potential in the written language often becomes more apparent when we read aloud, because the chosen words, the sound patterns that they create, and the physical demands on tongue and lips encourage us to breathe and enunciate in certain ways. A useful rule, therefore, when reading any Shakespeare play is to register those passages which are difficult to understand, or even physically to speak, and to ask not simply 'what does the character mean?', but 'what else does this very difficulty allow *me* to feel and think?'

Thus, in the longer speeches in which Leontes talks to himself, Shakespeare, by relying on the formal elements of rhythm and line length to connect words, almost abandons syntax. The three speeches beginning 'Too hot, too hot' (I.ii.150–208) repeatedly stop and start, changing direction and subject. This makes them particularly difficult to read silently. But this is because they are meant to show his confusion and his warped logic. The difficulty in meaning has in fact been compounded by editors and theatre directors who have tried to amend, repunctuate, or simplify the language so that it makes syntactical sense. But well performed, these false starts, sounds, and the gestures they demand or evoke, combine to simulate a window on his 'mind'. And, because they are spoken to us alone, they also make us complicit. We understand the full enormity of what he is imagining long before those imaginings begin to impact on the other characters. A similar process occurs in reverse in the statue scene, where Shakespeare's careful charting of the appearance of gesture, warmth and movement in the statue means that we keep pace with Leontes's responses. When at last we see him touch her, and hear 'O, she's warm' (V.iii.109), the emotional impact on us of that line, at that moment, is profound.

Statue, picture and print

The play contains the only reference Shakespeare ever makes to another artist: Giulio Romano (otherwise Giulio Pippi, c.1499–1546). Giulio was a pupil of Raphael and became chief artist, designer and architect to Federigo Gonzaga, Duke of Mantua. Giulio is not now known to be a sculptor, but his paintings and drawings all have extraordinarily sculptural, three-dimensional qualities, often termed 'mannerist'. His figures are frequently caught in energetic poses, as if on the point of moving or speaking. They are often depicted in an architectural setting, sometimes appearing to lean out of that frame, bridging the divide between painting and viewer. He is most famous for the Palazzo del Te, a suburban palace of pleasure built on the site of the family stables to house Federigo's mistress. This may have inspired Antigonus's otherwise bizarre statement that he will keep his stables where he lodges his wife (II.i.136–7), which in the play (as no doubt in Mantua) sets off a series of sexual puns on the idea of 'riding'. Giulio decorated the palace with extraordinary wall paintings, all involving life-size figures. One room shows the fall of the giants, and another, full-length portraits of many of Federigo's prize horses. A highly modelled drawing, which both shows the quality of his art and depicts personations also relevant to Shakespeare's play, 'Victory, Janus, Time and Gaea', is in the Getty Museum (www.getty.edu). Engravings of his work circulated in Italy, France and Flanders, and Prince Henry seems to have been a collector of mannerist art. Had Shakespeare seen such prints, he might well have thought that they represented statuary. He might also have read an epitaph, supposed to have been on Giulio's tomb (which has not survived), describing him as a sculptor, painter and architect. This can be found in the first edition of Vasari's *Lives of the Artists* (1550), although it is cut from later editions: 'Jupiter saw sculpted and painted bodies breathe and the homes of mortals made equal to those in heaven through the skill of Giulio Romano'. He may also have been aware of the scandalous publication, banned by the Vatican, entitled *I Modi*. This set of erotic sonnets by Pietro Aretino, illustrated by vigorously acrobatic and explicit drawings by Giulio, engraved by Marcantonio Raimondi, was certainly known, by reputation at least, to a number of other early seventeenth-century English writers. In this case, the Third Gentleman's line that Giulio 'so near to Hermione hath done Hermione' carries a sexual pun on 'done', as a subliminal reminder of the accusation against her, reinforced two lines later by the physicality of the phrase 'greediness of affection' (V.ii.99–101).

Critics have often pointed to the Clown's line that the crowd are 'going to see the Queen's picture' (V.ii.172) as evidence that Shakespeare was confused in his own mind about this artwork because he knew that Giulio was not in fact a sculptor. The word 'picture', however, is commonly used in contemporary financial account books for the life-size, fully clothed effigy of the deceased that invariably featured in early modern royal funerals in both England and France. The effigy or 'picture', with a face modelled and painted to look as lifelike as possible, and with eyes open in expectation of the resurrection, lay on top of the coffin during the funeral procession, but was afterwards erected in a standing position near the tomb. A collection of such effigies survives, albeit in poor repair, at Westminster Abbey. The bodies are roughly made on a wooden frame, padded with hay so that the clothes might hang properly, and with jointed limbs, enabling them to be dressed more easily, and to facilitate both lying and standing poses. They were hastily made in the month that commonly elapsed between death and the funeral, although a great deal of care was taken with the faces, which would usually be entrusted to an 'Italian master'. The statue in *The Winter's Tale*, by contrast, is supposed to be made of painted marble, and has been 'many years in doing' (V.ii.95).

The judgement that a painting or sculpture is so lifelike that it seems to be about to move or speak is a conventional expression of the highest praise for art during this period. Such skill and artifice were admired but also sometimes feared, as if it were only possible as the result of magic, although the moving statue, operated by hydraulics, was a feature of the latest Continental garden designs. Early modern writers commonly referred to the classical sculptors Praxiteles and Polycletus and the painter Apelles as the masters to which all artists should aspire, placing their skill in direct relation to the mythical story of Pygmalion, who falls in love with an ivory statue that he has carved. He prays to Venus for a woman just like her, before taking her to bed with him. The goddess, interpreting him correctly, brings the statue to life (Ovid, *Metamorphoses* Book X).

Exact likeness is also, of course, a marker of genetic inheritance: as Mamillius says 'I am like you, they say' (I.ii.209). This idea is also expressed in this play by the use of the word 'print'. Paulina takes the baby to Leontes:

> It is yours,
> And might we lay th'old proverb to your charge,
> So like you 'tis the worse. Behold, my lords,
> Although the print be little, the whole matter
> And copy of the father:
>
> (II.iii.96–100)

Sixteen years later, Leontes inevitably still obsessed with the same theme welcomes Polixenes's son with the words:

> Your mother was most true to wedlock, Prince,
> For she did print your royal father off,
> Conceiving you.
>
> (V.i.123–5)

The recognition that Florizel is the 'image' (l. 126) or picture of his father brings to his mind, and also to the audience's, a memory of Mamillius standing before him at the beginning of the play.

Art and artifice

Although the statue of Hermione is presented as first art and then magic, it turns out to be the natural, living, aging body of the character we know to be an entirely innocent and wronged woman. It was also, of course, in the early performances, played by a boy – or at least a young male actor. It is hedged about in the language of the play with ambivalence: it is an object of desire – a collectable – and of bodily appetite, 'lawful as eating'; it is also a poignant reminder of a lifetime of family happiness, and of family lives, that are irretrievably lost. It is capable of moving real audiences to real tears, yet it is the climax to what is probably Shakespeare's most conscious expression of the mechanics and quality of his own art.

Although the dialogue between Perdita and Polixenes at the sheep-shearing is commonly described as part of the age-old and enduring debate about art and nature, it is in fact more a debate about art versus artifice (see Commentary pp. 46–7). Perdita is not objecting to the art of grafting (and she knows the difference between grafting and taking cuttings, which Polixenes, in common with many critics, apparently does not). It is artifice and deceit that trouble her. Maybe that accounts for her silence on her return to her father's court. The girl who is embarrassed about dressing up, and does not want to paint her face, but who is neither ambivalent or reticent about sex and hopes to 'breed' with her lover (IV.iv.101–3) is now again in the place that had made her six or seven-year-old brother an expert in ladies' eyebrows (II.i.8–12). Were Shakespeare to have allowed her to speak, she could only have expressed her happiness, but that would have erased our memories of those other more painful things.

Shakespeare's play may purport to be an 'old tale', but its structure is actually highly experimental. It knowingly breaks all the rules, to the extent that it can still seem a challenge to perform. Its mixing of genres, however, matches its mixing of history and geography. It uses the Janus-faced ability of tragicomedy to look in different directions simultaneously as a structural principle, and it employs the traditional elements of romance to wring the heartstrings. It evokes terror against a background of silence, and joy to a range of different types of music. It ties all together through language: words and phrases in one half of the play echo or anticipate images and puns in the other half. It is the dramatist's answer to the then new and exciting arts of both perspective and landscape design.

In the autumn of 1610 Prince Henry had begun to redesign his palace and gardens at Richmond. He had probably already employed Salamon de Caus, whose treatise on the art of drawing perspectives and shadows would be dedicated to him (published in French in 1612) and whose later treatise on automata, statues moved by hydraulics, reflects both his plans for Richmond and some designs already executed for the Coudenberg Palace gardens in the Spanish Netherlands. After Henry's death, de Caus was almost immediately employed by Henry's sister and her new husband for the magnificent and fabled alterations to their gardens at Heidelburg.

De Caus used artifice to simulate nature. It was said that birds would smash themselves against the solid walls that supported his *trompe l' œuil* paintings of landscapes, thinking them to be real. By contrast, the no place that is the sea coast of Bohemia is a reminder that the natural world in this play is more unreal than that of the court. And yet it is there, thanks to the humanitarian values of the Old Shepherd, that a succession of court characters, all in various forms of disguise, are able to find themselves. Even Autolycus momentarily becomes almost honest against his nature. Shakespeare seems to be saying that he uses nature, the real bodies of actors, to create a world that is impossible, yet one that explores desperate human problems, and in its very artifice evokes intense personal memories, regrets, desires and felt emotions in we who listen and watch. Autolycus's song 'When I wander here and there, I then do most go right' thus seems an apt metaphor for this idiosyncratic, complex, but assured play.

Early performances at court

Shortly after James acceded to the throne of England in 1603, all the Elizabethan acting companies, formerly under the patronage of different aristocrats, were brought into the various royal households. Shakespeare's company, previously the Lord Chamberlain's Men, now became direct servants of the King. The Crown may have hoped that they might thereby be able to exercise greater political control over these companies, but the new arrangements also arguably gave the actors more financial security, and better protection from attempts by the City of London to curtail theatre. The professional theatre companies were traditionally allowed to give public performances on the grounds that this enabled them to practise for their ostensible main function, which was to provide entertainment at court. But now, during periods of plague, when all public gatherings were banned (in courts of law as well as in the theatres), the King's Men were paid for rehearsals as well as performances. In 1609, for instance, they were paid £120 for twelve performances the preceding Christmas, and £40 'for their private practise in the time of infeccion that thereby they mighte be inhabled to performed their service before his majesty in Christmas hollidaies'. The following year, they received £30 for six weeks of private rehearsals and £130 for thirteen performances, one of which was probably Shakespeare's *Cymbeline* and which, given the long periods of theatre closure that year, may not have had a prior performance in public. Perhaps more than was the case in Elizabeth's reign, Shakespeare was now expecting to write specifically, and first and foremost, for court performance.

The division of the royal household responsible for everything pertaining to the day-to-day and social life of the court was the Chamber. Its financial accounts reveal that there was a considerable amount of theatre activity at court in the years 1610–13, with payments to the Queen's Players, the Prince's Players, and the Children of the Queen's Majesty's Revels as well as to John Heminges who is invariably named as the payee for the King's Majesty's Players, Shakespeare's company. By 1611, Henry's younger brother, the Duke of York and future Charles I, and his sister Elizabeth were also patrons of theatre companies, although the accounts show that they also commissioned performances from the companies nominally attached to their parents.

Insistence on Shakespeare's singular creative genius has tended to obscure the fact that in his role as royal servant he might have been expected to produce work that fitted thematically into a specified programme of royal entertainment. Indeed, as the chief dramatist of the King's Servants, one of his duties may have been to advise those commissioning court shows to decide on the appropriate 'device' or theme. Court entertainments were regularly linked to each other within the season, and also from season to season in successive years. Once we start to look at other surviving texts specifically designed for performance at court during this three to four-year period from the investiture of Prince Henry as Prince of Wales to the marriage of the Princess Elizabeth, we can see some striking correspondences.

Ben Jonson's *The Masque of Oberon*, commissioned by Prince Henry, was performed at court on 1 January 1611. With its theme of Arthurian chivalry and passing mention of 'the pearl that Tethys wears', this masque glances back to Jonson's playlet introducing *Prince Henry's Barriers*, and to Daniel's masque *Tethys Festival*, both written for the festivities accompanying Henry's installation as Prince of Wales, and performed in January and June 1610 respectively. In turn, the *Barriers* play shares with *Cymbeline* a young woman asleep, presumed dead, in a cave in Wales.

Similarly, *The Masque of Oberon*, which, in its set and costume designs, continued the antique Romano-British theme found in the *Barriers* and in *Cymbeline*, undoubtedly has features that find their way into *The Winter's Tale*. *Oberon* opens with an antimasque. This had become a standard feature of the Jonsonian masque, and comprised a show of some kind of disorder performed by professional actors, presented so that it might be tamed or banished by the appearance of the courtiers taking the dancing, non-speaking, masquing roles. In this case, the antimasque is a gathering of eleven satyrs and their Silenus, an older figure who, as Jonson's own notes to his text explains, 'is ever the Praefect of the Satyrs', and who will therefore be costumed like them (although satyrs are part man, part goat, while Sileni usually have horse ears).

The line in the play, 'three of them ... have danced before the king' (IV.iv.335–6) probably indicates that Shakespeare's company had supplied some of the actors for this antimasque. While the aristocratic masquers usually paid for their own extravagant costumes, it was not unusual for professional performers to be given costumes in payment, which may account for the fact that twelve expensive satyr costumes could be available to the company. It also means that the description of the satyrs' dance found in the stage direction and dialogue in the masque probably also describes the performance in the play. Their 'antique' or antic dance was 'full of gesture and swift motion', while their 'shaggy thighs' are hung

> with bells
> That as we do strike a time
> In our dance, shall make a chime
> Louder than the rattling pipes
> Of the wood gods.
>
> *(Masque of Oberon)*

Their strange behaviour was also intended to be funny. Eyewitness William Trumbell (cited Orgel and Strong, *Inigo Jones*, 1973) stated that the 'satyrs and fauns had much to say about the coming of a great prince to be followed by a thousand benefits, in the hope of which the fauns [i.e. satyrs] danced about joyfully, exciting great laughter. They then danced a ballet, with appropriate music with a thousand strange gestures, affording great pleasure'.

A Sylvan guard to Oberon's palace then speaks a panegyric to James I, which echoes Jonson's earlier compliments to James in the shows performed at his coronation. James's virtues make time stand still, or herald a permanent return to a golden age of justice and perpetual spring:

> 'Tis he, that stays the time from turning old
> And keeps the age up in a head of gold.
> That in his own true circle, still doth run,
> And holds his course, as certain as the sun.
> He makes it ever day, and ever spring,
> Where he doth shine, and quickens every thing
> Like a new nature.

In Shakespeare's play, however, this power to make time behave in peculiar ways is invested in the main female characters, not in the King. Perdita, who looks so much like Hermione and brings spring back to Sicily, 'quickens' or enables both her parents to live again, while it is Paulina, not the King or indeed any of the male characters, who fights against tyranny.

Love freed, and love restored

Certain themes from *The Winter's Tale* are also to be found in the masques performed at court in the long run-up to Princess Elizabeth's marriage.

These include the moral superiority of pastoral and country sports; the concept of 'triumph' and, crucially, of love confined in a cold country but ultimately conquering both time and riches, breathing life into a statue. Dating the Queen's masques at this period indicates that *The Winter's Tale* may well have been one of the fifteen unnamed plays that Shakespeare's company performed at court between November 1610 and 2 February 1611, for which payment is recorded in the Chamber accounts. This was up to six months before Forman saw the play at the Globe.

At the beginning of December, the Venetian ambassador, Mark Antonio Correr, had reported that the Queen was also to present a masque that Christmas and that it was to precede the Prince's masque of *Oberon*. His subsequent reports show that her masque was intended to be used to entertain the French Marshal de Laverdin who was due to visit to sign a treaty, but that it was put off repeatedly for a variety of contradictory reasons: they are waiting for the Marshal to arrive but he is delayed by adverse winds; he is still in mourning (for the assassination of Henri IV) and has no wish to dance; it is delayed because they are waiting for him to depart; there is a fault with the stage machinery. The Queen tells him she hopes to perform it on Twelfth Night (6 January), and later that it was due on the Feast of the Purification, otherwise known as Candlemas (the official end of Christmas on 2 February). Finally, in a letter dated 1 February he says that it will take place 'the day after tomorrow', i.e. 3 February. That year this was the first of just three days available for the Shrovetide period of carnival between Candlemas and Lent.

The delayed masque was Ben Jonson's *Love Freed from Ignorance and Folly*. It consists of an antimasque in the form of a triumph over love, with a Sphinx, a personification of ignorance, leading Cupid bound as a captive. He will be freed if he can answer the Sphinx's riddle: to identify 'a world, the world without', an eye which is 'light and treasure too', and which 'still moves, and still is fixed', and possesses 'powers' in which are mixed 'two contraries', which neither time nor fate have previously been able to join. His failure to answer correctly prompts a wild dance of twelve she-fools. Love appeals to the ladies in the audience for help, but then twelve priests of the Muses dance and sing, which gives him the wisdom to answer correctly. Britain is the world; James, the eye, its sun; James's wisdom is fixed in his breast but moves to guide other people; majesty and love are the contraries, which he joins together. Love is freed, ignorance and folly banished. The masquers, consisting of the Queen and ten ladies, appear as the daughters of Aurora (dawn), and after various dances, a final song celebrates the triumph of beauty over ravaging time. The single stage design that can be associated with this event shows the ladies seated in majesty, above an Arthurian gothic castle, surrounded by clouds and surmounted by two cupids holding a garland.

There is no firm date for the companion piece to this masque, *Love Restored*, also by Ben Jonson, which occurs immediately after *Love Freed* in Jonson's *Works* published in 1616, and which is described as being performed by the King's Servants. Indeed, its antimasque is much more of a play than usual. It begins with Masquerado complaining that the production is in melt-down: the musicians are missing and 'the rogue play-boy that acts Cupid, is got so hoarse, your majesty cannot hear him'. Plutus, god of money, enters complaining about the 'vanity' of such follies. He too is a little boy, as indeed he was in Jonson's verses for James's coronation procession, and several times in the course of the show he is mistaken for Cupid. The sprite Robin Goodfellow now enters demanding whether there is going to be a masque or not. He asks this question several times, presumably addressing members of the court audience directly, no doubt to great comic effect. He complains that court sports are less impressive than the 'gambols of the country', and runs through his adventures in trying to gain admittance. He has disguised himself as a succession of tradespeople involved in the masque production, but the porters have refused him admission each time; 'they asked me if I were the fighting bear of last year, and laughed me out of that'. He came next as a citizen's wife – which resulted in being felt up by one of the court guards, 'groping of me as nimbly as the Christmas cut-purse' – and then as a foreigner, but was told he 'had English enough to carry me to bed; with which all the other statues of flesh laughed'. Eventually Cupid enters flanked by ten male masquers representing the virtues of the court.

There is something topsy-turvy about this masque. The presenter Robin Goodfellow is an aspiring masquer whose disguises highlight the deceitful nature of masquing itself, and the principal masquer, Cupid, is unusually a speaking boy actor, not a dancing aristocrat. Although a close companion to *Love Freed*, seemingly commenting on it, it does not read like a conventional masque. It would, however, be entirely suitable as a carnival show. This masque was dated to early in 1611 by John Nichols, but for the last hundred years it has been more often identified with a passing reference in the account books to a masque by 'the prince' for Twelfth Night 1612 on no other evidence than that a cutpurse had been arrested in the Chapel Royal that Christmas and was due to be executed. That particular event does not, however, match the humour in Robin's speech. By contrast, Jonson's 'groping' cutpurse tallies closely with Autolycus's gleeful account of meddling with wenches' plackets at the sheep-shearing (IV.iv.601–12).

Robin's confusion as to whether there is to be a masque or not exactly bears out Correr's descriptions of the repeated postpone-ments of the Queen's masque that year. Equally, his reference to the perhaps grimly humorous 'fighting bear of last year' must point to an unusual occurrence, and not just to one of the many bear-baiting shows at court for which theatrical impresario Philip Henslowe was being paid at this time. On 23 June 1610, the entire royal family had gone to the Tower to see the baiting of 'a great fierce beare which had kild a child that was negligently left in the beare-house. This fierce beare was brought into the open yard behind the lyons' den, which was the place for the fight; then was the great lyon put forth, who gazed awhile, but never offered to assault or approach the beare'. A succession of animals – mastiffs, a horse and 'diverse other lyons' – were each tried in turn. The lions 'skipt up and down and fearefully fled' but although the dogs attacked the horse and had to be taken off, none attacked the bear. On 5 July, 'according to the King's comman-dement this beare was bayted to death upon a stage; and unto the mother of the murthered child was given twenty pounds out of part of that money which the people gave to see the beare kild' (Nichols, *Progresses of James I*, vol. ii, 1828, p. 259).

The mixture of ludicrous frustration and sheer bloody terror in this story is analogous to that needed for the performance of the bear episode in the play. As is often remarked, a pair of well-behaved white bear cubs had been used to draw the chariot in which Prince Henry had made his entrance as Oberon in his masque, but the effect there must have been magical and charming. A real adult bear, as the inci-dent at the Tower indicates, would be too unpredictable. What was needed for the play was an actor in a bearskin (to which, it is clear, the theatres had ready access), who could time his actions to trigger both alarm and laughter in the audience.

The purpose behind these two masques of *Love Freed* and *Love Restored* is evidently to turn the court's attention away from the heroic celebrations of Henry's investiture as Prince of Wales to the question of his and his sister's marriages. The entertainments stress the importance of various types of love (the people's love for the royal family, the romantic love engendered by Cupid), over political alliance-making and finance. The English people, in the form of Parliament, were in fact resisting the Crown's demands for increased funds, and tensions were high. Indeed, Correr writes that on the proroguing of Parliament that year, the King had remarked that 'while parliament is sitting it is interregnum for him'.

In December, a letter to Ralph Winwood, who was then ambassador in the Netherlands, had mentioned plans for three masques that year: 'Yet doth the Prince make but one mask, and the Queen but two, which doth cost her majesty but £600' (15 December 1610, Winwood, *Memorials of Affairs of State*, iii. p. 239). Perhaps politically therefore, and perhaps from necessity, the Queen was being slightly less extravagant than usual. But perhaps too she was using her theatrical commission to comment adversely on political plans for her daughter's marriage. In *Love Restored*, Robin Goodfellow complains:

> 'tis that imposter Plutus, the God of Money, who has stolen Love's ensigns; and in his bellied figure rules the world, making friendships, contracts, marriages, and almost religion; … usurping all those offices in this age of gold, which Love himself performed in the golden age. 'Tis he that pretends to tie kingdoms, maintain commerce, dispose of honours, make all places and dignities arbitrary from him, even to the very country, where Love's name cannot be razed out, he has yet gained there upon him by a proverb, 'not for love or money'. There Love lies confined by his tyranny, to a cold region, wrapt in furs like a Muscovite, and almost frozen to death, while he, in his enforced shape, and with his ravished arms walks as if he were to set bounds and give laws to destiny.

The Chamber accounts show that the Princess Elizabeth's own lodgings were prepared for a masque sometime during January 1611. The preparations took just two days, and this and the location indicate a more modest performance, suited to the intimate, humorous tone of *Love Restored*, in contrast to the grand effects in the Banqueting Hall required for both *Oberon* and *Love Freed*.

Whatever the precise dates, the coincidence of themes between these masques and Shakespeare's play is striking. Both Shakespeare and Jonson seem to be working to a brief which involves the reconciliation of a series of opposites: loss and return; riches and love; dynastic stability and marriage; true service and the purchase of honours; winter and spring. Yet Jonson provokes laughter at the 'statues of flesh' and the 'Christmas cutpurse' just as he was to poke fun at both the ballad-singing cutpurse of *The Winter's Tale* and the 'servant monster' (Caliban) from *The Tempest* in his 1614 Induction to his play *Bartholomew Fair*:

> A civil cutpurse *searchant*; a sweet singer of new ballads *allurant*; and as fresh an hypocrite, as ever was broached, *rampant*. If there be never a servant-monster i' the Fair, who can help it? he says; nor a nest of antics? He is loath to make Nature afraid in his plays, like those that beget Tales, Tempests, and such like drolleries, to mix his head with other men's heels, let the concupiscence of jigs and dances reign as strong as it will amongst you; yet if the puppets will please anybody, they shall be entreated to come in.

Wonder-inducing moving statues were nevertheless to become ubiquitous at court in the run up to the Princess Elizabeth's marriage in February 1613. The theme is found in Ovid's *Metamorphoses* in the story of Prometheus, who 'breathed life into moulded clay', and the Propoetides 'who dared to deny the divinity of Venus', being 'the first to prostitute their bodies; and who were therefore turned by her into stone', as well as in Pygmalion, who fell in love with the ivory statue he had carved, praying to Venus for a woman just like her. As Leonard Barkan has put it, 'Life in Ovid's poem ... is in flux between stoniness and the life that may emerge from or dissolve into stone ... with a reminder that the stone remains within us' (Barkan, 'Living Sculptures', p. 643). The masque statues, in gold and silver, along with the presence of Plutus, and the references (from *Oberon* onwards) to the present age of gold and its fixation on money, as opposed to the classical Golden Age of peace and justice, transmute the financial tensions between Crown and Parliament into an expression of generous love – while acknowledging that those tensions still exist.

The stony theme was taken up even in sermons. James as corner stone was the subject of the sermon given at Whitehall by Bishop Launcelot Andrewes on 24 March 1611, which was both Easter day and also the anniversary of the King's accession to the English Crown. His text was Psalm 118. 22–4 'The stone which the builders refused is become the head stone of the corner. This is the Lord's doing; it is marvellous in our eyes'. Andrewes stresses that James's right to the throne is firm as stone. But in a tour de force of temporal significances, he connects the double celebration of Easter and 'King's Day' with the day, 5 November 1605, on which James and his family had been nearly assassinated, claiming that in saving them God had made it 'a very Easter day to you, though it were in November'. He describes people who 'plotted to have put you by, and to have had some other Head-stone, of their owne heweing out' claiming that 'their meaning was to undermine and to cast downe foundations and all; yea to have made a right stone of you and blowne you up among the stones, you and yours' (Nichols, *Progresses of James I*, vol. ii, 1828, pp. 409–10).

While I have argued that *The Winter's Tale*, Shakespeare's play on the theme of 'love restored' was probably first performed that previous Christmas, it may not be accidental, in the light of this sermon, that it was also performed on 5 November that year (the first performance for which we have a record), nor, even, that Andrewes's text the following Christmas was on 'the word made flesh'.

'Statues of flesh' and the marriage of the Princess Elizabeth

By the spring of 1612, the question of Elizabeth's marriage was the subject of intense speculation, but in May, much to Prince Henry's satisfaction, the choice settled on Prince Frederick of the Palatine, the leading German Protestant prince and an Elector of the Holy Roman Empire, who arrived in England on 16 October. The marriage was delayed because of Henry's death in November, but the betrothal was celebrated on 27 December and the marriage itself on Valentine's Day, February 1613. The match was not, however, to the Queen's liking. On 9 January 1613, the inveterate letter writer John Chamberlain wrote to Winwood, 'The Queen is noted to have given no great Grace nor Favour to this Match: and there is doubt will do less hereafter'. He also tells that one of Frederick's attendants gave out 'that his Master is a better Man than the King of Denmark [Anne's brother], and that he is to take place of him in the Empire, at least ways of a greater King than he, the King of Bohemia' (Winwood, *Memorials of Affairs of State,*

III p. 421; see p. 91 above). This was an aspiration that was to help keep
Shakespeare's play topical at court for many years.

A payment to John Heminges dated 20 May 1613 records that the
King's Men had performed fourteen plays before the Princess Elizabeth
and the Elector Palatine that winter. Unusually, it lists the plays, including *Much Ado*, *The Tempest*, *The Winter's Tale*, *Sir John Falstaff* (presumably *Merry Wives*) and *The Moor of Venice* (*Othello*). No fewer than three
masques were performed to celebrate the marriage itself, along with
a spectacular firework display involving St George slaying a dragon; a
sea fight between Christian and Turkish ships staged on the Thames;
and a tournament. Each of the masques includes rivalry in love, a tri-
umphant return to spring, and the bringing back to life of not just
one but a whole set of statues.

The *Lords' Masque* by Thomas Campion was performed on the marriage night itself. After an antimasque of Orpheus, Entheus (or poetic
fury), and those who have run mad for love, it involves the transformation of eight bright stars into eight masquers. They are presented
with 'four noble women-statues of silver'. An invocation to Jove suc-
ceeds in turning these into 'women fit for love'. In dance, the eight
men compete for the four women 'Each woman hath two lovers, / So
she must take and leave a man, / Till time more grace discovers'. Four
more women statues then appeared and were likewise transformed,
so that 'No man needs fear a rival in his love'. General dancing ensued,
until the scene was 'again changed, and became a prospective with por-
ticoes on each side'. In the middle was a tall obelisk of silver, a symbol of
fame and memory, and on either side 'standing on pedestals, were the
statues of the bridegroom and bride, all of gold in gracious postures'.
The whole contraption then moved forward to music, apparently
drawn on a golden thread by a sibyl, who in Latin celebrates Elizabeth
as the mother of kings and emperors, observing that the strength of
Britain has been added to that of Germany, two peoples with one
mind, one faith; both will have the same enemy, the same ally.

Both Plutus and statues returned in the antimasque to George
Chapman's *Memorable Masque*, performed by the gentlemen of Middle
Temple and Lincoln's Inn the following night. The conceit of Francis
Beaumont's *Masque of the Inner Temple and Grays Inn*, however, performed
the following Saturday is that Mercury is staging a celebration of the
union of two rivers, Thames and Rhine – representing the countries of the bride and groom. This concept had also formed a fleeting

reference in Chapman's masque. Iris scoffs that he has only provided a single-sex dance of nymphs. He responds by summoning statues from Jove's altar. These 'were attired in cases of gold and silver close to their bodies, faces, hands and feet, nothing seen but gold and silver, as if they had been solid images of metal'. They are only half brought to life for the first antimasque and 'retaining still somewhat of their old nature, giveth fit occasion to new and strange varieties both in the music and paces'. Iris now invokes Flora's aid to conjure up the second antimasque of comic country figures, a token that the royal marriage is 'blessed with the love of the common people'. Both antimasque dances pleased the King so much that he demanded an encore, although sadly, by that time, one of the 'statues' had got out of costume. Finally after fifteen Olympian knights are brought to life from a 'heavy trance' at the merest sight of the King and have been paired off with their ladies, the masque must end: Time cannot be stopped – although the fourth and final song wishes that once husband and bride are in bed 'And not a creature nigh them' they might 'catch his scythe, as he doth pass / And cut his wings and break his glass / And keep him ever by them'. Love conquers time yet again.

Some twenty years previously, Shakespeare had concluded his comedy *Love's Labours Lost* with death, the postponement of anticipated marriages, and the line 'The words of Mercury are harsh after the songs of Apollo'. Because of its royal theme, and the central importance that the characters place on Apollo's oracle, the sun ought to be the presiding deity of *The Winter's Tale*, just as the person of the sun king, James, is usually cited as the cause of beneficial transformation in the court masques. But instead, both in plotting and in language, the play is genuinely mercurial (see pp. 96–8 above), quick-footed, and constantly shifting – a feature not achieved in Beaumont's masque. It is this that allows *The Winter's Tale* to fit into the programme required for performance at court during that period while avoiding the panegyric of masque.

After her daughter and son-in-law left England for a triumphal journey across the Netherlands and Germany to Heidelburg, Queen Anne consoled herself by travelling to take the waters at Bath. She was entertained at Cawsome House near Reading with a series of entertainments by Thomas Campion, being met in the fields and gardens of the estate by a succession of cultivated rustics, and by Flora herself. Campion published this entertainment and his *Lords' Masque* in the same volume but in reverse order so that, as in Shakespeare's play, rusticity precedes the apotheosis of statue transformation.

The themes for Shakespeare's play are therefore central to the iconography surrounding the marriage of the Princess Elizabeth. Elizabeth's very name conjured memory of the dead Queen Elizabeth, while the young bride in the play is the lost princess of an island kingdom, whose true worth is recognised by a desirable foreign prince. The loss in the real royal family of a promising young prince, the importance of Bohemia in European politics, its growing relevance to the royal family once Frederick had been chosen as Elizabeth's husband, the constant threat of war, and the fact that the play can be read as having a hopeful romance ending, meant that its topicality was not merely retained but enhanced, thus explaining its continued popularity at court. In 1618 the Bohemians revolted against Emperor Ferdinand II, and Frederick accepted their offer of the kingship the following year. He and Elizabeth journeyed to Prague but remained King and Queen for a brief year before being ousted and sent into exile by the returning Emperor's forces, thus fulfilling Ferdinand's prophecy that Frederick would be a 'winter king', gone with the melting snow. It was the beginning of the Thirty Years War but James continued to maintain England's peace by abandoning his daughter. She and her husband lived out the rest of their lives in exile.

4   *Critical Assessments*

Perhaps the most important advice contained in Aristotle's *Art of Poetry* is that 'a poet should prefer probable impossibilities to improbable possibilities' (24.10). Everything about the story of *The Winter's Tale* from its geography to its statue is impossible, and throughout the play (not just in the closing scenes), characters tell us that the events they have witnessed or heard about are a source of wonder or surprise. But partly because of their recognisably real emotional responses, including laughing at what they see, and partly because, most of the time, we are ahead of them in terms of precise knowledge about those events, we accept those events as probable within the strange world created by the patterns in Shakespeare's language, and his plot – the *arrangement* of the story.

Reading for the story, and also for the beauty of the language (as until comparatively recently was the main function of literary criticism), critics have dwelt on the charms of Hermione and Perdita while tending to be nonplussed by the impossibility of that story, often attempting to impose sense on it by interpreting it as allegory. In both cases, interpretations often tell us more about the critic's own concerns or time of writing than they do about Shakespeare's.

Shakespeare's own warning to critics not to regard the gaps of time and place in the play as a 'crime' has been widely disregarded. Ben Jonson, his contemporary, lampooned the play (see p. 120 above), John Dryden and others writing in the Restoration period thought that Shakespeare's breaking of the classical rules was the result of the lack of a proper education. Alexander Pope in 1725 surmised that most of *The Winter's Tale*, apart from a few notable poetic passages, must have been written by somebody else, while the poet and critic Samuel Jonson who thought that pastoral was 'plain, easy, vulgar, and therefore disgusting', produced no more than a few unremarkable notes on the play in all his Shakespeare criticism.

Charlotte Lennox in *Shakespear Illustrated* (1753) was the first to dwell at
length on the supposed sudden onset of Leontes's jealousy, preferring
the treatment in what she calls Greene's 'novel'. The two *Florizel and
Perdita* plays staged in London in the mid-1750s (see pp. 131–4), however,
were immensely successful. They brought unity to the play by axing
the first three acts and are perhaps partly responsible for an enduring
critical tradition that tries to account for the impossibilities in all the
so-called 'late' plays (*Cymbeline, Winter's Tale* and *Tempest*) by labelling
them as 'romances'. In this context, the protean word 'romance' is
understood in the sense of sentiment and beauty, and shows little detailed
understanding of the Elizabethan romance genre, which combines quest,
struggle and heartache in an often miraculous setting. Shakespeare's
supposed infringements of classical rules, however, began to be seen
as a triumph of his natural, untutored 'genius', although this is usually
considered to be a genius of poetry and language rather than dramatic
construction. There are a number of early nineteenth-century paintings, some now in the possession of the Royal Shakespeare Company,
which revel in the prettiness associated with the play at that period.
One by Henry Thomson (1773–1843), which depicts the shepherds
finding the infant Perdita, has the overtones of a painting of the infant
Jesus in a stable; a lamb looks on while the old shepherd holds up the
bearing cloth to reveal the infant swathed in a bright white light. This
approach, combined with the popularity of James Frazer's *The Golden
Bough* (a study of pre-Christian vegetation myths and legend published
in 1890), has meant that for whole generations of critics, the play has
had no real-life or political connotation and was little more than a
beautiful essay in redemption, rebirth and regeneration, whether pagan
or Christian. This approach is exemplified in F. C. Tinkler's article for
Scrutiny (1936–7), E. M. W. Tillyard's *Shakespeare's Last Plays* (1938) and
S. L. Bethell's short book-length study of the play (1947). Indeed, to
Northrop Frye (*A Natural Perspective*, 1965), 'The mythical backbone to
all literature is the cycle of nature, which rolls from birth to death and
back again to rebirth'. Such approaches to this play, of course, tend to
gloss over the fact that Mamillius and Antigonus are not reborn, and
that for sixteen years Hermione has suffered a living entombment.

Anna Jameson in *Shakespeare's Heroines* (originally published as
Characteristics of Women, 1832) groups Perdita among the 'characters of
passion and imagination', relating her to Italian pastoral but also to
'warm, breathing, human loveliness'. She saw Hermione, as a 'character

of the affections', 'gentle, beautiful and innocent' and a model of 'con-
jugal submission, truth, and tenderness', comparing her not with the
mannerism of a Giulio Romano painting but with the delicacy of one
of Raphael's 'heavenly madonnas'. She remarks on Shakespeare's rare
artistic ability to 'dive into the profoundest abysses of character, trace
the affections where they lie hidden like the ocean springs, wind into
the most intricate involutions of the heart, patiently unravel its most
delicate fibres' in order to create a character of such calm 'dignified
self-possession'. Always, a sensitive and intelligent critic, Jameson
accepts that the character's sixteen year concealment is not 'probable
in itself, nor very likely to occur in everyday life', but she trounces the
unnamed writer who had objected that no such 'tender and virtuous
woman' would have been so unfeeling as to have made her husband
suffer for so long, once she was apprised of his repentance. For her,
the sequestration has 'all the probability necessary for the purposes
of poetry' and 'all the likelihood it can derive from the peculiar character of Hermione'. Her description of the effect of the statue has
not been bettered: 'an effect which at the same moment is, and is *not*
illusion … in which the feelings of the spectators become entangled
between the conviction of death and the impression of life, the idea
of a deception and the feeling of a reality'. Unusually, she also devotes
space to Paulina, 'a character strongly drawn from real and common
life … clever, generous, strong-minded, warm-hearted … fearless in
asserting the truth … regardless of the feelings of those for whom
she would sacrifice her life, and injuring from excess of zeal those
whom she most wishes to serve'. Perceptively she observes that the
two characters are never brought face to face in the play, 'for this
would have been a fault in taste, and have necessarily weakened the
effect of both characters'.

Despite several attempts to explain the play's structure as a tragicomedy, a lack of understanding that Elizabethans frequently used
mixed genres in a variety of pastoral and non-pastoral forms as a
vehicle for political commentary has meant that the approaches
to the play outlined above have continued to circulate in criticism.
A late twentieth-century explosion of interest in the Jacobean court
masque as simple propaganda and an expression of state power often
failed to identify the struggles for power that these entertainments
expressed, and did nothing to persuade critics that the play's use of
masque elements and a long-lost princess was not a straightforward

endorsement of divine monarchy. Similarly, the knowledge that Shakespeare's company had at last managed to obtain permission to use the indoor theatre at the Blackfriars led critics to state repeatedly that the obvious masque-like aspects of the play were due to the use of this theatre, despite the fact that the only known public performance was at the Globe. Those Shakespeareans whose work is largely in theatre history have also been reluctant to see Shakespeare's Jacobean plays in terms of his work for the court, or if they have done so, have not been able to reconcile this with the idea that that work might also be politically engaged and critical.

J. I. M. Stewart was the first of a succession of critics who have tried to argue for the reality of Leontes's jealousy by suggesting that the boyhood friendship between Leontes and Polixenes is a classic example of the psychogenesis of homosexuality as outlined by Freud. Several studies thereafter have looked for motivation for Leontes's state of mind in childhood trauma, separation from the mother, and sibling rivalry, none of which of course is shown or even reported in the play.

Michael Bristol writing in the early 1990s when greed was 'good', comments on the gold left with the baby as a 'financial endowment' that 'provides the conditions for the possibility of social reconciliation'. He thus sees what he terms 'Leontes's initial sacrifice' as a 'successful long-term investment. Time is indeed money here, and it is this element of time as a factor in strategic long-term calculation that redefines the spatio-temporal form of the play as the action draws to a close' ('In Search of the Bear', p. 166). He can see no reason for Hermione's reconciliation (if that is indeed what happens) with Leontes, but describes her 'resurrection' as 'the result of a strategic calculation on the part of Leontes'. Although this is 'initially conceived in terms of expenditure within the spatio-temporal realities of a gift economy', it is achieved 'by means of fiduciaries in the profoundly altered spatio-temporal realities of a market economy' in works of art. Apparently forgetting that it is Paulina who has commissioned the statue (or rather fed and clothed Hermione for sixteen years), he claims, 'Leontes's "redemption" is not brought about by grace and by forgiveness but is rather the result of his own bold, risk-raking decisions combined with his patience and enormous capacity for deferral'. Hermione, however 'has another story to tell', that of the 'intersubjective or dialogic fullness of time symbolized so powerfully in the gestation of the child in the mother's body'. This 'experience of co-presence in time and space' is 'the untold story … that has been systematically and violently excluded from the spatio-temporal organisation of the play.'

Russ McDonald also focuses on spatio-temporal organisation, but this time in the rhetorical structure of the language. He notes that the play's long, parenthetical sentences often withhold their point until the very end: 'What distinguishes *The Winter's Tale* is that much of the poetic language is organised periodically: convoluted sentences or difficult speeches become coherent and meaningful only in their final clauses or movements.' McDonald relates this thesis to Frank Kermode's insistence in *The Sense of an Ending* (1966, republished 2000) that one of the reasons why humans need literature is that it gives meaning to inchoate existence. McDonald asserts; 'a similar principle governs the arrangement of dramatic action: the shape and meaning of events become apparent only in the final moments of the tragicomedy' ('Poetry and Plot', 1985).

While the Commentary section to this book has pointed out that the full understanding for the reader or audience of phrases and events in the early part of the play indeed only becomes apparent in the light of the closing scene, it has also argued that the closing scene is only probable in the light of linguistic and dramaturgical structures set up by the dramatist right from the start. The sense of the particular beginning is therefore as important as the ending, while, as we have seen, the meaning of Leontes's inchoate speeches are conveyed to our senses and imaginations in the process of their being spoken, provided editors and actors allow that process to occur and do not try to impose grammatical sense on them too soon.

With the exception of B. J. Sokol's *Art and Illusion in the Winter's Tale*, which examines the play in terms of the more sophisticated approaches to art, iconography, and the philosophy of art current when Shakespeare was writing, most critics have been content to repeat unexamined the claim that the play is an expression of the traditional debate of art versus nature, not stopping to reconcile this claim with the fact that nature in this play is so clearly a product of art.

There are few other book-length studies of the play, and comparatively little attention given to it in more general books on Shakespeare. Most of the work has been done in little bits (reflecting single aspects of the play's contradictory nature) in short articles. Taken as a whole, this criticism demonstrates that the play itself is indeed an example of the Renaissance concept of *concordia discors*, but still begs the question that Theseus asks of the unintentionally comic tragedy of 'Pyramus and Thisbe' at the end of *A Midsummer Night's Dream* 'How shall we find the concord of this discord' (V.i.60). Maurice Hunt, however, in the introduction to his collection of essays representing the history of the play's criticism, does a remarkable job in describing the nuances in a criticism which has generally been too much shaped by the sense of the play as a redemptive 'late' work, the result of a man focussing on his own imminent death, rather than the experimental work of a man in the prime of an active, public and economic life as an entrepreneur in both art and business.

5   *Key Productions*

Writing in 1993 while reviewing Adrian Noble's Royal Shakespeare Company production of the play for *Shakespeare Survey*, Peter Holland remarked that he had never seen a successful production of *The Winter's Tale* on the Stratford stage. It seems that the critical approaches to the structure of the play have carried over into the theatre with directors unsure how to handle what they have often seen as a 'broken backed' text. The fact that Shakespeare's text mixes up geographical, historical and cultural details has, however, enabled theatre directors to present it as an allegory for the cultural concerns of their own period. And as with the masque of 1611, Leontes's cold kingdom has been as likely to suggest a snowbound Russia as an oppressive Sicily.

David Garrick, *Florizel and Perdita*, Drury Lane, 1756

At the Theatre Royal in Drury Lane, the actor manager David Garrick solved the problem of unity by cutting the first half altogether. Billed as a 'Dramatic Pastoral in three acts' *Florizel and Perdita* was first performed in 1756 (published 1758) in response to a similar adaptation entitled *The Sheep-Shearing: Or Florizel and Perdita* by Macnamara Morgan, which was proving a great success at the rival theatre, Covent Garden. The Prologue, written and spoken by Garrick, who was later to reappear as Leontes, compared the theatre to a tavern in which poets were the vintners. This particular theatre/tavern, he claims, is the 'Shakespeare's Head', the fountainhead of 'choicest spirits', unlike the rival establishment, Covent Garden, which he lampoons as the 'Tom Durfy's'. Thomas D'Urfey (1653–1723) was a dramatist, satirist and songwriter who had been responsible for a complete rewriting of *Cymbeline* as *The Injured Princess*. Garrick scornfully refers to those critics who cannot distinguish between sparkling perry and real champagne, and who mistake Durfy's adaptation for the real thing. He has to admit, however, that there is some perry mixed in his own production, since he is expanding the second half of Shakespeare's play to a full-length piece. Somewhat contradictorily, he claims that, although he is cutting the first three acts, he wants 'To lose no drop of that immortal man!' Accordingly, his version opens with a conversation between Camillo and some gentlemen in which Camillo announces that Leontes intends to visit his old friend the King of Bohemia, but is 'alarmed' on behalf of Paulina, 'that excellent matron' whose arrival is even more imminent. Garrick incorporates lines from the first three acts of Shakespeare's play as Camillo fills us in with the story of Hermione's 'dishonour' and the exposure 'by the king's command' of her baby daughter on the shores of Bohemia. Paulina now enters with Polixenes, who tells her to stop weeping, but left alone at the end of the scene, she tells us that her tears express her joy that, 'for her royal mistress' sake', she might shortly welcome a penitent Leontes to Bohemia.

In the next scene, the Old Shepherd and his son have just witnessed a fearful shipwreck. The Clown tells us that two 'poor souls' have been cast ashore; 'they are out-landish folk; their fine clothes are shrunk in the wetting' and are being given succour at the shepherds' cottage. It turns out later that these are Leontes and Cleomines. The play now presents the scene with Autolycus and the Clown, played in front of painted backdrops of the Bohemian coast and countryside. The scene then opens up to reveal 'A prospect of a shepherd's cottage'. This indicates that the full depth of the stage was flanked by a series of flats – full height canvas screens painted in perspective, perhaps edged with cut-out shapes representing trees and foliage, thus suggesting a receding avenue or prospect with a cottage in the distance. The text follows Shakespeare's for IV.iv. Perdita gives rue and rosemary to the disguised Polixenes and Camillo, and the 'hot' flowers of middle summer 'to others' (compare p. 47 above). Perdita, played by Mrs Cibber, however, sings a new song, set by Michael Arne, the text of which was reprinted numerous times during the eighteenth century in collections of popular songs from the theatres and London pleasure gardens and was retained in later productions in other theatres. This ditty, 'Come, come, my good shepherds, our flocks we must shear', delights in the 'Content and sweet cheerfulness' of the simple rustic life and is rather removed from the actuality of rural poverty in eighteenth-century England. The possibility that the Clown has had sex with Mopsa is made rather more explicit, and when he tries to hush the 'wenches', Dorcas complains 'I have heard old folks in the parish say, that some folks have been proud and courtly, and false-hearted ever since some folk's father found a pot of money by the sea-side here'. There is no dance of satyrs, but otherwise the scene is more or less intact until the shepherds and shepherdesses exit with Autolycus as he sings the song 'Will you buy any tape'?.

Leontes and Cleomines now enter from the cottage at the back of the stage, in borrowed shepherds' clothes. They therefore witness the Old Shepherd's attempt to perform the handfasting of Doricles and Perdita (whose beauty strikes Leontes forcibly and offers him some comfort for his grief). But when Polixenes reveals himself, Leontes cannot face him and moves away, leaning for support on Cleomines, though they still remain on stage. After Polixenes and Camillo leave the scene, Leontes takes on the role of adviser to the unhappy couple, employing some of Camillo's words from the corresponding scene in Shakespeare, but still with a fair amount of 'perry':

> Trust to my words, tho' myst'ry obscures 'em —
> I know the king your father, and if time,
> And many accidents (cease foolish tears)
> Have not effac'd my image from his breast,
> Perhaps he'll listen to me.

Garrick's Act III in 'Another part of the country' presents Autolycus 'in rich clothes' which he has stolen from 'four silken gamesters', members of Polixenes's entourage who have been 'revelling by themselves at some distance from the shepherds'. This solves the perceived problem of how swapping his clothes for Florizel's 'swain's wearing' in Shakespeare's version enables Autolycus to look like a courtier (compare p. 44 above).

The scene now switches to Paulina's house, where a Gentleman tells her about the meeting between Polixenes and Leontes, who 'on the sudden assum'd a majesty of mien and feature, that threw a kind of radiance over his peasant garb, and fixt all who saw him with silent wonder and admiration'. Camillo now enters, and in dialogue based on Shakespeare's V.ii, recounts how Perdita has been identified as the lost daughter of Leontes. Paulina sends Camillo with an invitation to view the statue of Hermione done by a 'most true master of Italy'.

A change of scene takes us to Polixenes's court for the meeting between Autolycus and the gentrified shepherds. The Clown asks for his hand and is put out when he finds it contains no bribe: 'am not I a gentleman? I must be gently consider'd' (cf. IV.iv.796). Autolycus gives him gold, telling us, 'I have brib'd him with his own money'.

The final scene takes place in the gallery of Paulina's house. Although it follows Shakespeare's text quite closely up to the unveiling of the statue, there are significant differences in affect and meaning. Florizel kneels with Perdita at the sight of the statue, and when Hermione embraces Leontes, Perdita 'leans on Florizel's bosom' as he remarks 'My princely shepherdess! This is too much for hearts of thy soft mould'. The biggest difference, however, is that any ambiguity concerning Hermione's feelings at being reunited with her husband is completely removed. She addresses him as 'husband' and when he asks 'have I deserv'd / That tender name'? replies, 'No more; be all that's past / Forgot in this enfolding, and forgiven'. The marrying off of Paulina to Camillo, is removed. Instead, Leontes tells her to 'Live bless'd with blessing others', and proceeds with the more important business of royal introductions. He presents Polixenes to Hermione, telling her explicitly to 'look upon my brother' (compare p. 76 above), commands Camillo to pay his duty to the royal group, commending his 'worth and honesty', and introduces Hermione to her future son-in-law. Perdita, meanwhile, is overcome with 'shame / And ignorance', fearful that she does not know how to behave like a lady. Florizel comforts her with

> Be still my queen of May, my shepherdess,
> Rule in my heart; my wishes be thy subjects,
> And harmless as thy sheep.

Charles Kean, the Princess Theatre, 1856

By contrast, Charles Kean's classical Greek setting for *The Winter's Tale* in 1856 was partly a response to a popular craze for the more fortune-hunting and exotic aspects of archaeology. In letters written to his historical adviser, the architect and editor of *The Builder*, Geoffrey Godwin, he explained that the play was to be set 'in the city of Pericles … when it had attained its greatest splendour in literature and art'. The production was accompanied by a conjectural recon-struction of ancient Greek music, based on (1776) Burney's *Dissertation on the Music of the Ancients Charles.*

Kean is aware that he is playing with epochs and places in order to reduce to consistency Shakespeare's own historical anachronisms – 'Delphic oracle, Christian burial, an Emperor of Russia, and an Italian painter of the sixteenth century' – and argues in his preface to the printed acting edition that it is 'permissible' to 'have adopted a period when Syracuse, according to Thucydides, had, from a mere Doric colony, increased in magnificence to a position in no way inferior to that of Athens herself, when at the summit of her political prosperity' (Preface pp. v–vi).

Although he was later elected to the Society of Antiquaries for his services in popularising archaeology, his voracious appetite for histori-cal detail, sometimes lampooned by his contemporaries, seems to have been governed by a strong visual, decorative sense. He wrote to Godwin saying that he had seen an engraving of 'The Tomb of Midas' with 'carving so peculiar and so beautiful that I should like to introduce it (that is the same pattern) on the walls of Polixenes' Palace'. Follow-ing a suggestion made earlier by Thomas Hanmer, he had amended Bohemia to Bithynia, arguing that 'the difference of name in no way affects the incidents or metre of the play'. The change not only gave him an evidently legitimate seacoast, but enabled him 'to represent the costume of the inhabitants of Asia Minor at a corresponding period associated so intimately with Greece' and with the additional advantage of 'close proximity to the Homeric kingdom of Troy'.

On another occasion, he worried: 'The only possible objection I could have to the scene you [Godwin] so kindly propose is the doubt that such a thing as a ruined temple with habitations worked into it existed at Athens during the period we have selected. I think the interior of a servant's, or rather, say, a mechanical's abode would be more appropriate. Surely we could find something like it among the remains at Pompeii?' The abodes of mechanicals could evidently be presumed to be less historically specific than those of their betters, for he was also at pains to warn Thomas Grieve, the set designer, that he should be careful not to introduce any hint of Roman architectural details into his vision of Athens.

Kean's insistence on the Athens of Pericles and her 'political pros-perity', however, signals more than just archaeological curiosity or aesthetics. The connection is made rather more explicit in a speech at the banquet on 20 July 1859 celebrating his retirement from management of the Princess's, which was laid on by fellow Old Etonians and widely reported in the press: 'Gentlemen, in the days of ancient Greece, the theatre and the drama were the most effective instruments in forming the character of that remarkable people'. This, together with Kean's claim to have produced 'less an exhibition of pageantry appealing to the eye, than an illustration of history addressed to the understanding' (Preface, p. x) is particularly suggestive when we consider that the entire third act of his version of *The Winter's Tale* comprises the trial of Hermione. The set for this scene was modelled on the great theatre at Syracuse, and was painted to look as if it were filled with people, supplementing the huge cast of real-life extras on the stage. Kean is at pains to explain in the printed edition of the play that legal trials did indeed take place in theatre buildings in ancient Greece, but the effect in performance must have been to suggest both that the theatre was the crucible of civic society, and that the people had a legitimate interest in the activity of their rulers and an opinion on injustice. The production choices, combined with a belief in Shakespeare's universal relevance, thus invite a consideration of Athens as the birthplace of democracy with the political development of those 'remarkable people' the English.

The conditions pertaining at Kean's time of writing and production include the nervous response by the English establishment to the year of revolutions in Europe in 1848 and, at home, the long drawn out, incremental process of the reform of Parliament and the extension of the franchise. Significantly, perhaps, the most exalted Old Etonian at the Kean farewell banquet was William Gladstone, then a minister in Palmerston's Conservative Administration, but a lifelong supporter of reform. As the magazine *Era* reported, 'the love of English people for the drama is second only to their love for liberty' (August 1859).

Harley Granville Barker, Savoy Theatre, London 1912

Although its significance was not appreciated at the time and it was not a financial success, the production by the immensely perceptive scholar and director Harley Granville Barker is arguably the single most important production of the play to date. Unfortunately the prompt book has disappeared, but the ethos of the production can be assessed through a number of costume designs, photographs, reviews and Granville Barker's own introduction to the play, sold as a pamphlet programme in the theatre.

In contrast to previous theatrical tradition, this production presented the play virtually uncut, using the pace of delivery, which that requires, to increase the comprehensibility of the overall structure of speeches. John Palmer, writing in the *Saturday Review* (23 November 1912), observed that Leontes 'delivered some of his speeches very rapidly, because they were speeches which are unintelligible if they are delivered slowly'. Visually too it attempted to match Shakespeare's play in its mix of modern and historic reference and its use of theatrical space. The backdrop was a set of curtains hung between simple square pilasters (removed for the second half of the play), but the stage was built out over the orchestra pit, with the innovation of lighting from above and from the auditorium rather than from footlights, thus enabling actors to address the audience direct. As George Bernard Shaw observed, 'Instead of the theatre being a huge auditorium, with a picture frame at one end of it, the theatre is now a stage with some unnoticed spectators round it' (*Observer*, 29 September 1912). Satyrs appeared in classically grotesque, oversized facial masks, and Giulio Romano was recruited as costume designer for the court scenes, albeit a Giulio mediated by the costumes for Diaghilev's *Ballet Russe* and the paintings of Matisse, Mondrian and Picasso seen in the second Post-Impressionist exhibition held in London in October 1912. In a photograph, Perdita stands in a belted shift dress with a bold geometric pattern (that would have revealed more leg had the actress not sewn it up), outside a cottage, or rather a bungalow, which though thatched, reflects the garden suburb movement's attempts to improve the quality of workers' dwellings.

Barker was struck by the fact that no other play of Shakespeare's 'boasts three such women'. As Dennis Bartholomeusz puts it, 'If the set was "decorative", the costumes "mythical", the characters were approached, to start with, in the spirit of realism' (*The Winter's Tale in Performance*, 1982). But Barker also dared to take 'Exit pursued by a bear' literally, with an actor in a bear skin and simulating a bear-like gait, chasing Autolycus round and off the stage. It is undoubtedly this mixture of styles, which combined with the staging and pace of delivery, gave the production its life.

Trevor Nunn, Royal Shakespeare Company, 1969–70

Some of the features of Barker's production can also be found in Trevor Nunn's:

> At the beginning Christopher Morley's 'period' costumes for Leontes and Hermione are white like most of the outfits for the same designer's Hamlet at Stratford this year ... when we join up again with Leontes, he and his court are dressed in a manner that suggests a space-age, planet-hopping assembly of the future.
>
> (Plays and Players, September, 1970)

The head of wardrobe reported in the local press: the bear 'is made of goatskin with expanded polythene on a bamboo frame. It is a splendid specimen. The actor will have to wear special eight-inch high boots to lumber across the stage' (*Birmingham Post*, 16 May 1969). The intent seems to have been to terrify with stroboscopic lighting effects, but the reviewers' responses are amused 'the whole calamity has a nice turn of speed, and an even nicer blend of visual elegance and nonchalant absurdity' (*The Spectator*, 23 May 1969). The sheep-shearing was a 'flower-power hippy festival' and the satyrs dance seemed to many reviewers to take its cue from the line 'men of hair' to import a 'rave-up' from the musical *Hair*, although it seems that Nunn had not seen that show. Judi Dench played both Hermione and Perdita to great acclaim, although critics also observed that the switch-over in the middle of the statue scene was distracting and detracted from the emotion of the reunion between mother and daughter, since of course Dench as Hermione was then playing to a body-double.

Declan Donnellan, Cheek by Jowl & Maly Theatre, 1999

In conversation with Peter Holland (*Shakespeare Survey*, 2003), Declan Donnellan reported that he had wanted to do *The Winter's Tale* with the Russian Maly theatre company because they were mostly in their forties and he felt that the play was about people of a parental age, looking back. Although he had recently been happy to direct *King Lear* with a very young training company for the RSC, he felt that *Winter's Tale* needed the weight that older actors could provide. The

Russian context also allowed him to make direct political comparisons. The opening scenes seemed to reviewers to recall the court of
Tsar Nicholas II, but Hermione's trial had 'unmistakable allusions' to
the Stalinist show trials of the 1930s. It was clear (as indeed it is in the
text of the play) that the oracle was irrelevant to the outcome; the
verdict had already been decided and the trial was merely a show of
justice prior to passing sentence.

Donnellan observed:

> one of the reasons that Shakespeare is a great writer is because he knows
> that words don't work and you have to know that words don't work before
> you can write properly because it's believing that words work perfectly
> that gets us into so much trouble ... These expressions, these means of
> communication, are fantastic precisely because the author knows they
> don't work perfectly, that they are inadequate to express feeling.
>
> (*Shakespeare Survey*, 2003, p. 162)

Nevertheless, he had difficulty approaching the second half of the play.
Charles Spencer, writing in the *Daily Telegraph* (10 May 1999) found
insufficient difference between Sicily and Bohemia: 'the set consists
of bare wooden blocks making a floor and back wall, and four chairs.
And, er, that's about it. There is something irritatingly self-conscious
about this visual parsimony'. Not content with the subtle doubts
about reconciliation and future happiness expressed in the play
through Hermione's silence towards her husband, this production
also cut much of the end of the final scene, including the pairing up
of Camillo and Paulina.

Edward Hall, Watermill Theatre, Newbury 2005

Edward Hall's production for The Watermill, Newbury in Jan–March
2005 (later touring to the US) was one of a series of Shakespeare productions by his Propeller Theatre Company using all male casts (see
pp. 104–5 above). Several reviewers commented that the appearance
of the male actors – their large hands and feet – brought attention to
the vulnerability of women in a man's world:

> You are overwhelmed by how isolated these women are in this world of
> powerful kings and lords. That they are played by men makes the truth

of female isolation all the more shocking. Then the actors move and speak. They become one with the action. You realize that theater is always about transformation and that transformation is always a process.

(Margo Jefferson, *The New York Times*, 4 November 2005)

The production became an investigation of the problems of fatherhood and family breakdown, seen through the eyes of the young prince Mamillius, since the actor playing this part also acted Time and Perdita. It opened with sand falling steadily from an hourglass 'in the sky'; a 'small pyjama-clad boy plays with his wooden dolls, screwing up his eyes against the terrors of the night'. His toys marked the action, with a wooden ship reflecting his baby sister's voyage to Bohemia. Leontes' court was 'frosted with ice and thick with the smug smell of cigars and brandy. ... Jealousy strikes here like a hot flush in a cold white light. It is swiftly followed by madness – the madness of men who cut themselves off emotionally from their wives and children.' (Lyn Gardner, *The Guardian*, 28 January 2005)

All the reviewers delighted in the actors' knockabout 'puerile impersonation' of sheep, and Autolycus's 'Northern rocker', who managed to divest the 'Young Shepherd of his entire wardrobe' (Paul Taylor, *The Independent*, 4 February 2005), although several noted that it was a mistake to cut Polixenes's speech on art and nature. At the end, Perdita removed her frock and reverted to Mamillius, recoiling from Leontes 'as if he has had a nightmarish vision of the man he may become and rejects it. If there is any redemption here, it is a ghostly one' (Gardner). Alastair Macaulay's review in the *Financial Times* is a fitting summary of both production and play:

Somehow it does not matter that *The Winter's Tale* is more complex than any single production can fully realise. As with so much of Shakespeare, we find our breath taken away by the originality of its human relationships, its theatrical situations, its violent emotions and above all its piercing imagery, so that to return to the play in the theatre is often to feel we are experiencing it for the first time (2 February 2005).

6 The Play on Screen

Considering the dearth of modern films of the play, it is perhaps surprising that there might be as many as four silent film versions: by Edison (1909); the Thanhouser film company (1910, 12 minutes, 35 seconds, reissued on DVD); the German Das Wintermärchen, by Belle Alliance (1913–14), about which almost nothing is known, and which may therefore bear no more resemblance to Shakespeare's play than the title; and Tragedia alla Corte di Sicilia by the Italian Milano company, distributed in England as The Lost Princess (1913, 34 minutes). The Milano version was very well received at the time, and is credited as being the most successful film adaptation of Shakespeare prior to World War I. The *Kinematograph and Lantern Weekly*, 15 March 1914, reported that it 'is splendidly acted, magnificently staged, and photographically beautiful' and although taste in acting style has changed, the photography still appeals. The story is carried by 44 subtitles, but in a silent movie, verbal jokes are impossible and the character of Autolycus is understandably cut entirely. The death of Antigonus is accomplished by having him set upon by robbers rather than a bear, and thrown into a volcano. This not entirely successful attempt at spectacle was shot on red film stock, with other night-time sequences shot on green stock. Book-ended by scenes of Shakespeare reading his play to a couple of friends, the film adds scenes to the story of Hermione, who is threatened with madness by the loss of her baby. It also attempts to rationalise her sixteen year disappearance by showing Paulina purchasing and administering a 'potion to save the life and reason of her mistress', as the subtitle explains, before, like Juliet in *Romeo and Juliet*, she is buried in a tomb.

The story of Perdita is correspondingly truncated. Since there is no Autolycus, the identity of the pretty shepherd's daughter is established immediately after the angry unmasking of Polixenes at her 'rustic betrothal'. Trying to establish his innocence, the Old Shepherd displays one of the coins that he had found with the child, which bears Leontes's head and the motto, 'Leonte Rex Siciliae'. Polixenes and Camillo return with Perdita to Sicily. The reunion of the two kings, and Leontes's recognition of his daughter, which in the play take place offstage, are given two separate scenes in the film. Leontes then wants to show Perdita 'the face of her mother'. The tomb is opened to reveal nothing but a robe. In Paulina's house, Hermione is presented not as a statue but as apparently dead. A subtitle announces 'The awakening of Hermione', although this is not shown (or does not survive), and the sequence presents only the happy reunion of Leontes, Perdita, Hermione and Paulina. The story ends with a long shot of all the characters before returning to Shakespeare finishing his reading.

A twenty-six minute version of the story, with a screenplay by Leon Garfield and directed by Stanislas Sokolov was included in the series *Shakespeare: The Animated Tales* (1994). Anton Lesser, Jenny Agutter, Sally Dexter and Michael Kitchen provided the voices of Leontes, Hermione, Paulina and Polixenes respectively.

A French film, *The Tale of Winter (Conte d'Hiver)*, written and directed by Eric Rohmer, and part of his *Tales of the Four Seasons* seems tangentially related to Shakespeare's story. It concerns a young woman who has a holiday romance, loses contact with the man but bears his child, and five years later, still in love with him, is living with the little girl in Paris, trying to decide which of her current two lovers to choose. This tale of desire for a lost love, however, also characterises the three other films in the series, and indeed Rohmer's work in general.

There have been two versions of the play made for BBC TV. The first by Don Taylor with Sarah Badel as Perdita (1962), and the second by Jane Howell for the BBC Shakespeare Series (1981). Howell was also responsible for the three *Henry VI* plays, *Richard III* and *Titus Andronicus* in that series. Her *Winter's Tale* begins with a ball sailing over the high, stylised, white hedge of a wintry garden and bouncing at the feet of Camillo and Archidamus, to their amusement, as they stroll down a long alley leading to a cobbled circle. This is surrounded by more white, clipped hedges, over-peered on one side by the sprawling bare branches of an ancient tree. It is like the centre of a maze, and its exits are guarded by clipped pyramidal bushes. Howell employs considerable depth of field, and repeatedly shows characters approaching from a long way off, sometimes behind the group that is talking in the foreground. Many of Leontes's comments are delivered direct to camera while his attendants hover in the background. The set, staging and camera work combine to give a powerful sense of a cold, controlled society, a place in which privacy is impossible, and surveillance likely, although Mamillius is oblivious to this, and runs around happily except when confronted by his father in I.ii. Most of the characters are dressed in black; Leontes has a rich dark fur collar and hat, suggestive of black bear, but Hermione and Polixenes are in shades of buff: he, rather louche and unlaced; she, elegant in a gown trimmed with what might be finest lambskin. Mamillius wears a tawny-green, skirted coat and matching hat.

The set remains essentially the same for the second half, although the formality is broken up. The infamous bear is presented by the briefest shot of a rearing snarling animal. The tree is now hung with autumnally golden leaves, which turn to spring-like green when the scene returns to Sicily. Although the stylisation in the set saves the Bohemia scenes from being simply pretty, they suffer a little from the mummerset rusticity that so often creeps into productions of the play, and cannot accommodate the wild sexuality of the satyrs' dance, which has been cut. Generally, however, the artificiality of the setting acts as a foil to the emotional truth of the language, which is well and clearly spoken. The statue scene is genuinely moving.

There are also a couple of screened versions of stage productions: Frank Dunlop's adaptation of his 1966 Edinburgh Festival production with Jane Asher as Perdita and the wonderfully comic actor Jim Dale as Autolycus and one of Greg Doran's production for the RSC, recorded on the Barbican stage, and widely praised for Anthony Sher's performance as Leontes (TV direction by Robin Lough, 1999). Although recorded directly from the stage over two performances, this has translated extremely well to TV. The set and costumes designed by Robert Jones were inspired by photographs of the early twentieth-century court of Tsar Nicholas I. One photograph of a panelled long gallery with tall windows but no roof was seized upon as the visual key to the whole production. Removing the windows created a receding deep space with multiple entrances on either side, which director and designer thought of as the recesses of Leontes's mind. The ceiling was filled in with yards of billowing silk – something of a trademark of this particular director at that period. The effect is lush, and the colour scheme a symphony in greys, with the slightest touch of purple in Leontes's waistcoat, but the painted panelling was deliberately distressed and showing its age. As the story unfolds the walls were pushed slightly more together, enhancing the effect of length.

The production is, however, marked by a sometimes excessive interest in medical symptoms. Alexandra Gilbraith's Hermione, in the late stage of pregnancy is more breathless, waddling and ungainly than most women manage, and in common with other productions in the 1990s she appears at her trial with roughly cut hair and dirty, sweaty, grey gown, exciting gasps and murmurs from the standers-by, and prompting the officer to order 'silence' (see pp. 30–1, 144). This costuming was meant to indicate that she was utterly bereft, beyond the desire to live, but it undercuts the collected, proud composure of her speech and rather suggests that her women have not been doing their duty. A sickly Mamillius (Emily Bruni, who also doubles as a rather gutsy Perdita) is in a wheelchair from the beginning, perhaps explaining to a modern audience his sudden death, and giving pathos rather than humour to his line 'No my lord, I'll fight' (I.ii.163). But, in the characters' studied obliviousness to the boy's condition and the tension this sets up with their descriptions of him, it also suggests a pathological sickness at the heart of his parents' marriage.

More justifiably, Antony Sher, through conversation with a number of medical practitioners, identified Leontes's mental state as 'morbid jealousy' (see pp. 106–8 above). But the production is over-balanced towards that as diagnosis. At Hermione's trial, he takes out a crumpled piece of paper on which his opening speech is written and, because of the sleep deprivation associated with the condition, has difficulty in reading it. A false start is followed by an immense pause in which he folds and reopens the paper, usurping the silence that the play gives to Hermione in this scene. At last he reads, in a slightly rushed monotone.

The swirls of silk hanging from the flies are let fall for the storm and then, pushed from behind, become a huge enveloping presence suggesting that the bear has been underlying the set throughout. Then, lit with bright white light, they become the sheets and hangings of an immense bed, out of which pops first Autolycus and then a succession of country doxies. This Bohemia is a dirtier, sexier world than we normally see. Huge bales of wool are being stacked in a barn by well-muscled, leather-aproned farm hands at the beginning of the sheep-shearing, and the dance of the satyrs by men with horns on their heads, and outsized baggy trousers, each sporting an erect penis, creates a folkloric sense of combined threat and humour. Polixenes, however, while talking to Camillo in IV.ii indulges in a more effete kind of work: cross-pollinating a pair of different coloured orchids held by a couple of uniformed gardeners, as preparation and explanation for his argument with Perdita on pied gillyvors (IV.iv.81–100).

Ongoing preoccupation with Leontes's illness rather than Hermione's strength also seems to have shaped the staging of the statue scene. Just as Hermione's behaviour in the first scene seemed designed to show her to us through his eyes, so now it shows us what he was demanding: a pose of unconditional rectitude with head and eyes downcast, in the habit almost of a nun. The result, for this viewer at least, is distinctly unmoving.

Further reading

Editions

Orgel, Stephen, *The Winter's Tale* (Oxford: Oxford University Press, 1996).

Snyder, Susan and Deborah T. Curren-Aquino, *The Winter's Tale* (Cambridge: Cambridge University Press, 2007).

On *The Winter's Tale* and Shakespeare's later plays

Bloom, Harold (ed.), *Shakespeare's Romances* (Philadelphia: Chelsea House, 2000).

Bristol, Michael D. 'In Search of the Bear: Spatiotemporal Form and the Heterogeneity of Economies in The Winter's Tale', *Shakespeare Quarterly*, 42 (1991), pp. 145–67.

Egan, Robert, *Drama within Drama: Shakespeare's Sense of his Art in King Lear, The Winter's Tale, and The Tempest* (New York and London: Columbia University Press, c. 1975).

Frey, Charles, *Shakespeare's Vast Romance: A Study of The Winter's Tale* (Columbia and London: University of Missouri Press, 1980).

Hunt, Maurice (ed.), *The Winter's Tale: Critical Essays* (London: Garland Publishing Inc, 1995).

King, Ros, *Cymbeline: Constructions of Britain* (Basingstoke: Ashgate, 2005).

McDonald, Russ, 'Poetry and Plot in The Winter's Tale,' *Shakespeare Quarterly* 36 (1985), pp. 315–29.

——, *Shakespeare's Late Style* (Cambridge: Cambridge University Press, 2006).

Muir, Kenneth (ed.), *'The Winter's Tale': A Casebook* (London: Macmillan, 1968).

Overton, Bill, *The Winter's Tale* (Basingstoke: Macmillan, 1989).

Ryan, Kiernan (ed.), *Shakespeare: the Last Plays* (London: Longman, 1999).

Sanders, Wilbur, *The Winter's Tale* (Brighton: Harvester, 1987).

Shannon, Laurie, *Sovereign Amity: Figures of Friendship in Shakespearean Contexts* (Chicago and London: University of Chicago Press, 2002).

On tragicomedy and romance

Cooper, Helen, *The English Romance in Time: Transforming Motifs from Geoffrey of Monmouth to the Death of Shakespeare* (Oxford: Oxford University Press, 2004).

Henke, Robert, *Pastoral Transformations: Italian Tragicomedy and Shakespeare's Late Plays* (Newark: University of Delaware Press, 1997).

Newcomb, Lori Humphrey, *Reading Popular Romance in Early Modern England* (New York: Columbia University Press, 2002).

On performance

Bartholomeusz, Dennis, *The Winter's Tale in Performance in England and America, 1611–1976* (Cambridge: Cambridge University Press, 1982).

Draper, Ronald P., *The Winter's Tale: Text and Performance* (Basingstoke: Macmillan, 1985).

Warren, Roger, *Staging Shakespeare's Late Plays* (Oxford: Clarendon Press, 1990).

On masques, art, effigies and landscape

Barkan, Leonard, '"Living Sculptures": Ovid, Michelangelo, and the Winter's Tale', *English Literary History*, 48, 4 (Winter 1981) pp. 639–67.

Harvey, Anthony and Richard Mortimer (eds), *The Funeral Effigies in Westminster Abbey* (Woodbridge: Boydell Press, 1994).

Morgan, Luke, *Nature as Model, Salamon de Caus and Early Seventeenth-Century Landscape Design* (Philadelphia: University of Pennsylvania Press, 2007).

Orgel, Stephen and Roy Strong: *Inigo Jones: The Theatre of the Stuart Court* (London: Sotheby Parke Bernet; Berkeley: University of California Press, 1973).

Sokol, B. J., *Art and Illusion in The Winter's Tale* (Manchester: Manchester University Press, 1994).

Verheyen, Egon, *The Palazzo del Te in Mantua: Images of Love and Politics* (Baltimore: John Hopkins University Press, 1977).

Historic sources

Kean, Charles, *Shakespeare's play of The Winter's Tale. Arranged for representation at the Princess's theatre, with historical and explanatory notes* (London: J. K. Chapman, 1856). Kean's letters to Godwin are bound into a presentation copy of this edition in the Folger Library.

Lamazzo, Giovanni, tr. R. H., *A Tracte Containing the Artes of Curious Paintings* (Oxford: Richard Haydocke, 1598).

Nichols, John, *The Progresses, Processions, and Magnificent Festivities, of King James the First* (London: J. B. Nichols, 1828).

Winwood, Ralph, Sir, *Memorials of Affairs of State in the Reigns of Q. Elizabeth and K. James* I ed. Edmund Sawyer (London: W. B. for T. Ward, 1725).

Index